Connecting the Disconnected

DIRECTIONS IN DEVELOPMENT
Finance

Connecting the Disconnected

Coping Strategies of the Financially Excluded in Bhutan

Cecile T. Niang with Mihasonirina Andrianaivo,
Katherine S. Diaz, and Sarah Zekri

THE WORLD BANK
Washington, D.C.

Contents

Figures

Tables

Acknowledgments

This report owes much to colleagues at the Royal Monetary Authority of Bhutan, especially Madam Eden Dema, deputy governor, and her team, and members of the Financial Inclusion Policy Working Group. The team would like to thank Takao Takahashi, Namgay Dorji, and Dechen Choden from the Royal Monetary Authority for their technical inputs during the design, data collection, and analysis of the Bhutan Financial Inclusion Focus Group Survey. The team would also like to thank Pema Dechen Dorjee and Tshering Dema from the Royal Monetary Authority and representatives from Bhutan National Bank Limited, Bhutan Development Bank Limited, and T Bank Limited for providing data on the banking sector. The report benefited from guidance from Stefan Staschen, the Royal Monetary Authority's international adviser for the Financial Inclusion Policy. The survey was made possible thanks to the dedication and diligence of Ugyen Lham and her team at Druk Associates, the survey firm selected to undertake this work. The team would also like to thank the Bhutanese women and men who patiently responded to the survey.

The methodology and tools of the survey and the final report were developed with guidance and technical inputs from World Bank Group colleagues: Winston Dawes, Aurora Ferrari, Michael Goldberg, Giuseppe Iarossi, Aphichoke (Andy) Kotikula, Rafael Keenan Mazer, Ann Rennie, Mehnaz Safavian, and Siegfried Zottel. Katherine Scaife Diaz and Siegfried Zottel undertook technical reviews of the fieldwork, providing feedback to the survey firm. The team owes particular appreciation to Robert Saum, Ivan Rossignol, and Anthony Cholst for overall guidance and review.

The report is based on four community reports and a final country synthesis report produced by Druk Associates, with inputs from the Royal Monetary Authority and the World Bank. Katherine Scaife Diaz adapted Druk Associates' final country synthesis report to produce the initial draft of this report, identifying additional evidence from the community reports. Sarah Zekri and Cecile Thioro Niang wrote chapter 1, Mihasonirina Andrianaivo and Sarah Zekri chapters 2 and 6, Katherine Scaife Diaz chapters 3 and 4, and Sarah Zekri and Katherine Scaife Diaz chapter 5. Mihasonirina Andrianaivo designed and undertook a rapid survey of the banking sector in Bhutan and contributed the technology sections to all chapters. Sarah Zekri tirelessly identified good-practice design tools to inform the survey. Alison Strong provided editorial support. Cecile Thioro Niang coordinated, edited, and led the survey and report work from the World Bank side.

About the Authors

Cecile Thioro Niang is a senior economist in the South Asia Region Finance and Private Sector Development Unit of the World Bank and a country sector coordinator for Bhutan. Her work has spanned South Asia, Africa, the Caribbean, North America, and Europe. Her policy and research experience in financial inclusion includes microfinance, small and medium-size enterprise finance, partial credit guarantees, business development services, and financial literacy. She has published papers related to financial inclusion in Bangladesh, Bhutan, Nepal, and Pakistan. She holds degrees in economics, business administration, and information systems from Columbia University, University of Paris Dauphine, and Telecom Business School.

Mihasonirina Andrianaivo is a financial sector specialist in the South Asia Region Finance and Private Sector Development Unit of the World Bank. Previously she was an economist in the General Secretariat of France Telecom–Orange in Paris. Her work has focused on competition issues in the telecommunications sector as well as mobile financial services and their potential regulation, both in Europe and in African countries. She holds a Ph.D. in economics from the University of Rennes 1, focusing on banks, financial markets, and growth in developing economies. She has written several papers on issues related to financial development, financial structure, and mobile financial services.

Katherine Scaife Diaz specializes in qualitative research and analysis on topics that include financial inclusion, small and medium-size enterprises, migration and development, and community engagement. She has undertaken fieldwork throughout Latin America. In addition to the World Bank, she has consulted for Broad Branch Associates, the Inter-American Dialogue, and the International Finance Corporation. She holds a master's degree in law and diplomacy from the Fletcher School at Tufts University and a bachelor's degree from the University of Chicago.

Sarah Zekri has worked for the World Bank since 2004, focusing on financial sector development. She has field experience in Bulgaria, Haiti, Kosovo, and Latvia. She has supported and co-led investment lending operations in Kosovo and the Kyrgyz Republic and a development policy loan in Latvia and has participated in Financial Sector Assessment Programs in Algeria, Bulgaria, Haiti, and Latvia. Before joining the Bank, she worked for the United Nations Economic Commission for Latin America and the Caribbean and at HSBC Investment Bank as an emerging markets economist. She holds a master's degree in economics from the University of Paris Dauphine.

Abbreviations

ASCA	accumulating savings and credit association
ATM	automated teller machine
BDBL	Bhutan Development Bank Limited
BIL	Bhutan Insurance Limited
BNB	Bhutan National Bank Limited
BOB	Bank of Bhutan Limited
CGAP	Consultative Group to Assist the Poor
Druk PNB	Druk Punjab National Bank Limited
GDP	gross domestic product
GGLS	group guarantee lending scheme
G20	Group of Twenty
NGO	nongovernmental organization
NPPF	National Pension and Provident Fund
NSB	National Statistics Bureau
Nu	Ngultrum
RICBL	Royal Insurance Corporation of Bhutan Limited
RMA	Royal Monetary Authority of Bhutan
ROSCA	rotating savings and credit association
RSEBL	Royal Securities Exchange of Bhutan Limited
SBI	State Bank of India
SMS	short message service

Currency Conversion

Currency conversions in the report are based on an exchange rate, valid as of November 28, 2012, of 1 ngultrum (Nu) = US$0.018003.

Executive Summary

In the spring of 2012, the Royal Monetary Authority of Bhutan and the World Bank commissioned a diagnostic assessment of financial practices and strategies among urban and rural Bhutanese. The resulting survey, the Bhutan Financial Inclusion Focus Group Survey, represents one of the first efforts to capture household financial management practices in the country. The assessment, undertaken at the request of a government working group led by the Royal Monetary Authority, was designed to inform Bhutan's Financial Inclusion Policy by providing information about households' use of and demand for financial services.

Since the research mainly captures the perspectives of Bhutanese households, this report does not present recommendations. Instead, its findings from the field research provide qualitative evidence that has informed the Financial Inclusion Policy by highlighting opportunities and challenges in increasing financial inclusion.

Three Key Patterns in the Use of Financial Services

Three key patterns arise from the analysis of results from focus group discussions and in-depth interviews.

Bhutan is a cash-based economy where households have a vibrant, if informal, savings and lending culture. Households' financial management strategies remain informal, with formal financial services only weakly integrated into daily life. The lack of financial infrastructure such as point-of-sale devices outside cities reduces Bhutan to a cash economy. Since cash is the predominant form of exchange, people have fewer incentives to store money in banks or other financial institutions. When the formal financial system fails to offer a convenient service tailored to people's needs, informal strategies for savings, credit, remittances, and insurance fill the gaps.

Rural areas are particularly underserved. Use of formal financial services is particularly weak in rural areas of the country, where banks are distant and banking culture poorly reflects people's needs. But financial practices in rural Bhutan are beginning to resemble those in urban Bhutan: Rural Bhutanese are moving away from bartering and are receiving payments in cash rather than in labor. Housing scarcity across the country has generated investment interest among rural people. Families' interest in educating their children (and investing in the financial products that might help pay for their children's education) is as high in rural areas as it is in urban areas. The greatest difference in financial practices between urban and rural communities is that opportunities to save or invest in rural communities are infrequent, often depend on the harvest, and generate less wealth. Small, infrequent savings, coupled with poor access to banks, limit incentives for rural Bhutanese to obtain formal financial services.

Women and youth represent an untapped market segment. Women represent an opportunity to extend financial inclusion, because they are integrated into family businesses and appear more willing than men to try new technology. Rural women often take charge of bringing the harvest to market at a nearby city, where they manage the money from sales and make purchases. And women tend to be knowledgeable about the financial products available to them. Nevertheless, the share of rural women who reported using formal financial services is smaller than the share of rural entrepreneurs or farmers—male and female—who reported doing so. The lack of financial services directed to women overlooks the tradition of matrilineal property rights, in which women own and inherit land.

Youth feel excluded from the formal financial system, though more will gain access as they grow older. The exclusion of youth is indicative of a broader exclusion of the poor, landless, and informally employed. The ability of young people to leverage their skills and abilities to earn income will depend in part on access to formal financial services. Efforts to tailor financial services to their needs could help stimulate the economy by putting more youth and unemployed to work.

Key Findings of the Field Research

Fieldwork provided data to inform the recommendations of Bhutan's Financial Inclusion Policy (highlighted in appendix A). Key findings are summarized here and detailed in the report's chapters.

Financial Products Are Not Responsive to Households' Needs

Fieldwork identified a demand for financial services with less complex and time-consuming bank procedures, particularly in the following areas:

- *Small, periodic savings and loan services.* Savers and borrowers expressed a need to deposit or borrow small amounts of cash periodically throughout the year. Seasonal loans with repayments tied to the harvest or the sale of products would better reflect household cash flow and improve the likelihood of on-time repayments.
- *More accessible deposit and withdrawal services.* Depositing cash in banks is inconvenient for rural households, since there are no automated teller

machines (ATMs) nearby allowing them to withdraw the cash when needed. Deposit mechanisms in the local community that accept small amounts and keep the cash accessible for later use would encourage account uptake.

- *Flexible loan requirements.* Survey respondents expressed interest in loans that are not based solely on fixed assets collateral, that offer flexible term lengths, and that allow deferred repayment periods. There was also much interest in expanding opportunities to receive education loans beyond households with a salaried employee.

In response to the demand for saving locally and in small amounts, group savings schemes and cooperatives are slowly emerging in Bhutan, mainly in the form of welfare associations (*kidu tshogpas*). Savings clubs are run by community members who understand the savings capacity of contributors, allowing participants to save small amounts of money. Some of the savings groups are also planning to lend out the mobilized funds to their members. Contributing savings to the groups is considered faster and more convenient than making deposits in banks. There is an opportunity for savings clubs and cooperatives to serve rural communities until financial infrastructure or innovations in technology incorporate households into the formal financial system. In the meantime, support and capacity building for club management will be critical to ensure that households' savings are protected.

A lack of knowledge about insurance services appears to impede their use. While the Bhutanese are required to purchase life and home insurance, they rarely purchase other insurance products. Few people are aware of the types of insurance available to them, such as health, livestock, and travel insurance. If more people understood insurance products, there would probably be greater demand in the market for a tool that protects well-being during times of hardship. Awareness-raising campaigns could highlight the benefits of insurance, explain the claims procedures, and clarify consumers' rights and responsibilities.

Bhutanese households use remittances primarily to send money to family members within Bhutan and to students living in India. Outflows dominate international remittances, driven by the use of remittance services by households with family members abroad. Among formal remittance channels, commercial banks and Bhutan Post are the most frequently used. But many rural communities lack access to formal remittance services and must rely instead on informal—and often expensive—service providers.

Increasing women's financial inclusion will require a more precise understanding of their needs as well as financial products that reflect those needs. Smaller loan and deposit sizes could help in better matching products to women's needs. Women favor more frequent repayments and smaller installments that better correspond to their income cycles. In addition, young Bhutanese feel that collateral-free loans for youth education would improve their prospects for future employment and earnings and increase their self-confidence and financial integration.

Households Struggle with Banks' Loan Requirements—and Turn to Informal Lenders

Banks' requirements for high levels of collateral—in particular, fixed assets collateral—are among the main barriers that respondents identified in accessing financing. Assets accepted as collateral are limited to secured pledges, which can exclude many people from access to formal bank loans. Although a central registry is being established for secured transactions, there is no registry for movable assets, which would provide additional safeguards for lenders and expand opportunities for borrowing based on movable collateral.

In the absence of formal microfinance services, many Bhutanese households rely on informal lenders to fill gaps in the financial sector—turning to these lenders for quick, small loans for investment capital or for emergencies and immediate needs. Family, friends, and moneylenders appear to be by far the most common sources of informal small loans for households. Most households that borrow from informal providers do not attempt to borrow from financial institutions, mainly because bank products do not meet their needs. Even households with some access to the formal financial sector continue to use informal financing mechanisms.

Because informal lending is illegal in Bhutan, however, the processes and procedures for accessing an informal loan go unregulated. The findings of the field research highlight a need for formal microfinance services providing small group and individual loans with flexible repayments across all four geographic communities covered. Households may have access to some nongovernmental organizations (NGOs) that provide financial services, but many potential clients for microloans prefer to rely on savings or borrow from informal lenders.

Greater Financial Literacy and Consumer Protection Are Needed

The savings strategies and attitudes among respondents suggest that Bhutanese households could benefit from financial literacy education, particularly in budgeting and cash flow. Though respondents identified long-term savings goals, households' strategies to reach those goals are not consistent or well established; saving is an afterthought rather than the first step in financial management. Poor financial management skills make it more difficult for households to know when they will reach their savings goals, and can delay the attainment of those goals. Efforts to increase financial management skills among the Bhutanese are likely to also improve their ability to access formal financial services.

Financial consumers in Bhutan also need more effective consumer protection safeguards. Focus group discussions pointed to a nonconfrontational culture in which clients may accept ill treatment or look for opportunities to switch banks rather than confront bank officers who have treated them inappropriately. Households would welcome consumer protection mechanisms that take these cultural values into account, allowing them to obtain redress in a nonconfrontational manner. Most consumers are unaware of the consumer protection mechanisms now in place. And those who are aware of the option of pursuing recourse through a lawsuit view it as a costly and time-consuming solution that is not worth the effort. A clear and direct pathway for dispute resolution that is easily accessed would greatly increase trust in the financial sector. Survey respondents also highlighted a need for financial institutions to make policies and other materials widely available in local languages.

Technology Offers an Opportunity to Expand Financial Access Points

The mobile phone and Internet technology available in Bhutan does not appear to be driving financial inclusion. While mobile phone banking has revolutionized banking in countries with difficulties in financial access similar to those in Bhutan, its outreach has been constrained by the limited mobile banking technology in use and by the low English-language literacy in Bhutan. The only financial services available through mobile phone banking are text messages in English. But the widespread use of mobile phones suggests that innovative technology could create opportunities for greater use of mobile phone banking. Internet penetration is much lower, reducing interest in Internet-based banking services.

Respondents use ATMs to check account balances and withdraw cash. But they expressed dissatisfaction with ATM services, reflecting poor functioning of the services or perhaps their own poor understanding of how the services work. Poor understanding of how services function is a fundamental barrier that limits the potential for expanding financial access through improved technologies in Bhutan.

These findings on the current role of banking technologies in Bhutan, coupled with the scarcity of bank branches in its rural areas, suggest that other innovative strategies may also be worth considering. Branchless banking—whether based on bank agents or nonbank agents such as the postal network or businesses—is one solution for improving financial access in remote areas.

CHAPTER 1

Introduction

In the spring of 2012 the Royal Monetary Authority of Bhutan and the World Bank commissioned a diagnostic assessment of financial practices and strategies among urban and rural Bhutanese. The resulting survey, the Bhutan Financial Inclusion Focus Group Survey, represents one of the first efforts to capture household financial management practices in the country. This qualitative survey was carried out through focus group discussions and in-depth individual interviews in four Bhutanese communities in March–April 2012.

Objective and Context for the Survey

The assessment, undertaken at the request of a government working group led by the Royal Monetary Authority, was designed to inform Bhutan's Financial Inclusion Policy by providing information about households' use of and demand for financial services.[1] Building on the assessment's analysis, the draft Financial Inclusion Policy draws out policy objectives, strategies, and an action plan to increase financial inclusion while following some guiding principles (see appendix A for a summary of how this report's findings, along with global good practices, inform the draft policy). The draft policy reflects Bhutan's application of internationally accepted practices, principles, and standards of inclusive finance such as the Key Principles of Microfinance of the Consultative Group to Assist the Poor (CGAP 2004) and the G20 Principles for Innovative Financial Inclusion (GPFI 2011).[2]

The efforts of the Royal Government of Bhutan to develop a financial inclusion policy are not unique. Other countries also have developed financial inclusion policies and reforms—including Brazil, India, Indonesia, Kenya, and Peru. Appendix B describes how these five countries have successfully applied the G20 Principles for Innovative Financial Inclusion.

The survey's findings were supplemented by complementary analysis from the World Bank and two supply-side surveys of the financial sector:

• A just-in-time supply-side survey conducted by a World Bank team in June 2012, with the Royal Monetary Authority and with three commercial banks representing about 60 percent of commercial banking assets in Bhutan—Bhutan Development Bank Limited (BDBL), Bhutan National Bank Limited (BNB), and T Bank.

• The Supply-Side Access to Finance Survey, a survey of financial institutions in Bhutan conducted by BDBL for the Royal Monetary Authority in January 2012 to explore access to financial services (see RMA 2012). BDBL was mandated to undertake the survey as one of the members of the Financial Inclusion Policy Working Group.

By synthesizing results from focus group discussions and in-depth interviews, this report aims to improve the understanding of access to finance in Bhutan and identify household practices and preferences that provide opportunities and challenges in increasing financial inclusion. The report does not provide a full picture of financial inclusion in Bhutan. Doing so would require additional steps (box 1.1).

Qualitative Survey Methodology

The choice of the qualitative method for the survey of households' financial practices and strategies was motivated by the need for evidence that would feed into the tight timelines for the development of the Financial Inclusion Policy (see appendix D). Once available, results from the module on access to finance in the Bhutan Living Standard Survey 2012 will supplement the findings discussed here by providing nationwide quantitative data on households' access to financial services (see NSB forthcoming).

Site selection was based on a methodology developed for a Rapid Qualitative Assessment completed in Bhutan in January 2011 to inform the World Bank's *World Development Report 2012: Gender Equality and Development*. Four districts were selected on the basis of their socioeconomic characteristics and geographic distribution:

• Thimphu—an urban, economically vibrant district containing the capital of Bhutan
• Mongar—an urban, less economically vibrant district
• Paro—a rural, economically vibrant district
• Samtse—a rural, less economically vibrant district

Thimphu and Paro are located in the west, Mongar in the east, and Samtse in the south. Within each district a community was selected for the survey. In each community, focus group discussions were held with women as a separate group, young adults, entrepreneurs and both employed and self-employed people, and subsistence farmers and unemployed people (see appendix E for the survey field guide). Both women and men were interviewed in the non-gender-based groups. Two in-depth individual interviews were carried out within each demographic

---

Box 1.1 Topics in Bhutan's Financial Sector Not Covered by the Report

Supply-side data. This report focuses on demand-side information, providing limited information on providers of financial services. To get a full picture of access to finance in Bhutan, the Financial Inclusion Policy Working Group commissioned a survey of the banking sector to collect supply-side information—the Supply-Side Access to Finance Survey. Further quantitative and qualitative information would help in monitoring the implementation of the Financial Inclusion Policy—in particular, information on the evolution of the structure of Bhutan's financial sector, its financial depth, and indicators of banks' soundness (profitability, capital adequacy, and efficiency). A financial intermediation and access analysis would illustrate the evolution of access to formal financial services in Bhutan. Also useful would be an impact evaluation of government initiatives promoting financial access for households and small businesses.

Rupee shortage and the banking sector. Bhutan has experienced rapid credit growth in recent years (see box 5.1 in chapter 5). There has been a growing concern that credit expansion may have led to rising imports from India, resulting in deterioration in Bhutan's external position and fueling the rupee shortage in the country. This rapid credit growth may have led to greater vulnerability in the banking sector. Banking liquidity has shrunk, suggesting that financial institutions are less able to withstand shocks to their balance sheets and meet deposit withdrawals without facing liquidity problems. Portfolio quality could also become a concern. The rapid credit expansion may reflect poor credit decisions. Compounded by increasing macroeconomic vulnerability due to the rupee shortage, this could lead to serious deterioration in portfolio quality in the medium term. An in-depth analysis of vulnerabilities of the financial system is warranted, including stress testing to assess the resilience of banks to various risks or external shocks and a crisis preparedness exercise tailored to Bhutan, with the objective of supporting the authorities' institutional capacity to deal with financial crises.

Results of the Bhutan Living Standard Survey 2012. The Bhutanese authorities commissioned a third Living Standard Survey to gather data on households. The survey was undertaken in March–May 2012 and is expected to be released by the end of March 2013. This is the first Living Standard Survey in Bhutan to include a set of data on household access to finance (for the financial inclusion questionnaire, see appendix C). These national data will provide baselines for monitoring the implementation of the Financial Inclusion Policy and provide access to statistically significant trends in access to finance.

Access to finance by small and medium-size enterprises. The Bhutan Financial Inclusion Focus Group Survey focused on household access to finance. Demand- and supply-side information on access to finance for enterprises is covered in the 2009 Investment Climate Assessment by the World Bank (2010).

---

group to supplement the information collected through the focus group discussions.

At each survey site the field coordinator selected focus group participants before survey activities were conducted, using a combination of social networks in the communities and the contacts and suggestions of local authorities.

Table 1.1 Number of Participants in Each Focus Group Discussion in the Four Bhutanese Communities

Community	Young adults	Women	Entrepreneurs, self-employed	Farmers, unemployed	Total
Chengmari (Samtse district)	10	10	12	10	42
Mongar (Mongar district)	10	10	10	13	43
Thimphu (Thimphu district)	11	10	10	11	42
Shaba (Paro district)	10	12	10	12	44
Total	41	42	42	46	171

The selection of focus group participants was aimed at reaching a broad range of respondents but was often limited by the distance of potential respondents to focus group sites and their willingness to take time away from work.

In total across the four communities, 171 respondents participated in the focus group discussions and 32 in the in-depth individual interviews (table 1.1). The team also approached officials in banks and local administration offices to cross-check information and gather background on the communities.

This report's analysis draws on the World Bank's reference framework for financial inclusion strategies, prepared by its Financial Inclusion Practice for Mexico's 2012 G20 Presidency (World Bank 2012; also see appendix D). The framework identifies three aspects of a comprehensive assessment of financial inclusion: *access* (the financial products and services available to consumers), *use* (how much or how often consumers use the products), and *quality* (consumers' ability to benefit from the financial products on the market). Taking information about all three of these aspects into account can help ensure that a financial inclusion strategy moves beyond creating new financial products and services and instead leads to products and services that respond to financial consumers' needs.

Notes

1. Members of the working group include the Royal Monetary Authority, commercial banks, noncommercial banks, government ministries, mobile network operators, and nongovernmental organizations with an interest in microfinance. The working group presented an advance draft of the Financial Inclusion Policy to the Cabinet in early June 2012. The adoption of the policy is pending.

2. Nine core principles for promoting financial inclusion form the basis of the G20's Financial Inclusion Action Plan: leadership, diversity, innovation, protection, empowerment, cooperation, knowledge, proportionality, and framework (World Bank 2012).

References

CGAP (Consultative Group to Assist the Poor). 2004. "Key Principles of Microfinance." http://www.cgap.org/sites/default/files/CGAP-Consensus-Guidelines-Key-Principles-of-Microfinance-Jan-2004.pdf.

GPFI (Global Partnership for Financial Inclusion). 2011. "G20 Principles for Innovative Financial Inclusion." http://www.gpfi.org/sites/default/files/documents/G20%20Principles%20for%20Innovative%20Financial%20Inclusion%20-%20AFI%20brochure.pdf.

NSB (National Statistics Bureau). Forthcoming. *Bhutan Living Standard Survey 2012 Report*. Thimphu: NSB.

RMA (Royal Monetary Authority of Bhutan). 2012. "Supply-Side Access to Finance: Key Findings." Paper presented at a meeting of the Financial Inclusion Policy Working Group, Thimphu, April.

World Bank. 2010. *Bhutan Investment Climate Assessment Report: Vitalizing the Private Sector, Creating Jobs*. South Asia Region, World Bank, Washington, DC. http://documents.worldbank.org/curated/en/2010/09/16409092/bhutan-investment-climate-assessment-report-vitalizing-private-sector-creating-jobs-vol-1-2-volume-summary-report.

———. 2011. *World Development Report 2012: Gender Equality and Development*. Washington, DC: World Bank.

———. 2012. *Financial Inclusion Strategies—Reference Framework*. Washington, DC: World Bank. http://siteresources.worldbank.org/EXTFINANCIALSECTOR/Resources/282884-1339624653091/8703882-1339624678024/8703850-1339624695396/FI-Strategies-ReferenceFramework-FINAL.pdf.

CHAPTER 2

Financial Service Providers

A brief review of financial service providers in Bhutan and the array of services they offer to clients provides useful background for the results of the Bhutan Financial Inclusion Focus Group Survey on households' financial practices and strategies. Financial service providers in Bhutan can be broadly categorized as formal financial institutions (banks and nonbank financial institutions), informal moneylenders, and semiformal providers such as NGOs and cooperatives. In addition, Bhutan Post provides remittance services. The formal financial sector has undergone recent transformations and modernization but remains bank led.

Formal Financial Service Providers

Bhutan's financial sector has undergone rapid changes since 2009, notably with the entry of three new banks and one private insurance company. Five banks operate in Bhutan: two incumbents—Bank of Bhutan Limited (BOB) and Bhutan National Bank Limited (BNB)—and the three new banks—Druk Punjab National Bank Limited (Druk PNB), T Bank, and Bhutan Development Bank Limited (BDBL). Banks offer credit facilities, savings or deposit services, insurance, remittance services, foreign exchange services, and other financial services such as ATM services, mobile (SMS) banking, and internet banking.

BDBL is mandated by the Royal Government of Bhutan, which owns 93.7 percent of its capital, to operate in rural regions of the country (box 2.1). BDBL grants around 99 percent of the formal loans going to the agricultural sector (RMA 2012). Commercial financial institutions remain mostly concentrated in urban areas, viewing rural operations as unprofitable because of high costs and low profits. The predominance of lending based on fixed assets collateral further reduces the demand for services in rural areas, since rural clients often lack sufficient collateral or large savings in a bank.

Three nonbank financial institutions provide insurance and pension services: the Royal Insurance Corporation of Bhutan Limited (RICBL), the newly licensed Bhutan Insurance Limited (BIL), and the National Pension and Provident

Box 2.1 How BDBL Serves Rural Bhutanese Communities

BDBL operates a network of 29 mobile banking branches that offer group guarantee lending schemes (GGLSs) in rural communities. These schemes are aimed at overcoming the barrier that collateral requirements represent for rural clients by having group members stand as surety for one another. To deliver the services in remote communities, BDBL staff visit each community once a month, at a place, time, and date agreed on in advance with the community. Innovations such as BDBL's mobile banking products and services can help rural residents overcome savings and financing constraints.

Fieldwork found that service delivery differs across communities, however. Among focus group participants in Mongar, farmers from the villages of Tongsing and Jaibab considered BDBL to be very active in their community. They reported that in their community BDBL staff collect deposits and loan payments, disburse loans, assist people in filling out forms, and provide advice and other financial services. By contrast, participants in other communities reported that while BDBL staff come to their community once a month, they only collect deposits and loan payments. BDBL managers claim that they are unable to provide a full range of services in some communities because of the lack of photocopying machines or cameras that take passport-size pictures in the area. In border regions it is too dangerous for staff to travel with cash.

Even in the communities with access to BDBL's mobile banking branches, the very poor remain excluded from the services. GGLS loans are typically small and designed to share risk across several community members. But very poor community members often cannot find other group members willing to seek a loan with them. Poor women who own no land, or who are divorced or a single parent, also have little chance of being included in a loan scheme, because of other members' perception of their risk.

Communities and individuals, whether they have access to the formal financial sector or not, often turn to the informal sector for financing. Informal lenders therefore play a crucial part in expanding borrowing opportunities to the poor and marginalized.

Source: Bhutan Financial Inclusion Focus Group Survey 2012.

Fund (NPPF). RICBL is the dominant service provider, though BIL has quickly captured a large share of the market in its three years of operation. Uniquely, nonbank financial institutions in Bhutan—insurance companies as well as pension boards—are allowed to engage in lending activities. These institutions were initially allowed to lend because of the small market size and limited avenues for investment. But the concern that growth in private sector credit has translated into increased imports from India, fueling the rupee shortage, led the Royal Monetary Authority to reorient the activities of nonbank financial institutions and to suspend their lending. According to the Royal Monetary Authority's most recent monetary policy statement (June 2012) and directives on discontinuation of lending activities sent to nonbank financial institutions, they are to stop lending by June 1, 2014.

Bank assets have been growing steadily, tripling in size between 2005 and 2011, though they declined slightly in 2011 (figure 2.1). Assets of nonbank financial institutions have also grown. But the financial sector remains dominated by banks, which account for almost 90 percent of total financial sector assets (excluding the stock exchange). The stock exchange, the Royal Securities Exchange of Bhutan Limited (RSEBL), is shallow, with only 21 listed companies. Liquidity is low, and trading days are limited to three a week.[1]

The Royal Government of Bhutan has taken recent steps to modernize the financial sector infrastructure. In 2009 the Royal Monetary Authority established the Credit Information Bureau of Bhutan. Its aim was to increase the efficiency and reliability of the financial system by improving credit risk assessment, reducing the extraordinary amounts of collateral often required, lowering default risk, and enabling the expansion of credit-based lending. In addition, an electronic funds transfer and clearing system was inaugurated in June 2010. And to allow for the interoperability of ATMs and bank point-of-sale terminals, the Royal Monetary Authority launched Bhutan Financial Switch, a national card switch system, in December 2011.

Figure 2.1 Financial Sector Assets in Bhutan, 2005–11

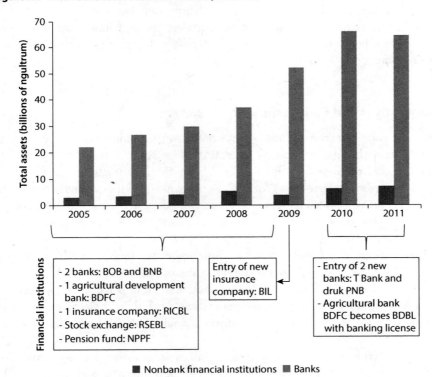

Source: Royal Monetary Authority of Bhutan.
Note: Data exclude RSEBL. BDBL = Bhutan Development Bank Limited; BDFC = Bhutan Development Finance Corporation; BIL = Bhutan Insurance Limited; BNB = Bhutan National Bank; BOB = Bank of Bhutan; NPPF = National Pension and Provident Fund; PNB = Punjab National Bank Limited; RICBL = Royal Insurance Corporation of Bhutan Limited; RSEBL = Royal Securities Exchange of Bhutan Limited.

Informal Financial Service Providers

Unlike formal financial service providers, informal providers typically only offer loans, though anecdotal evidence suggests that a few informal lenders may also accept deposits. Informal providers can be broadly categorized into two groups: moneylenders (individuals or businesses) and family members, relatives, friends, or neighbors. Moneylenders are typically wealthier community members. In rural areas informal lenders may include former government officials and retired public servants, corporate employees, community leaders and officials, senior monks (*dragays*), lay monks, religious institutions, and monastic bodies; in urban areas they may include contractors, large business owners, civil servants, corporate employees, businessmen, and gamblers. More than 200 informal lenders operate in one rural community in Samtse, working from within Bhutan and from neighboring India. This suggests that informal creditors dominate the market in communities where banks have little presence.

Focus group discussions suggested that the use of informal service providers is common among the Bhutanese, especially when they are seeking credit. But two issues made gathering information on informal lending a challenge: First, informal lending is illegal in Bhutan.[2] And second, informal loans can be considered shameful for families. Respondents in focus groups and individual interviews were somewhat unwilling to speak about personal experiences with informal lending practices.

Cooperatives and Civil Society Organizations

Few civil society organizations or intermediaries provide financial services in Bhutan, and there is no formal microfinance sector. Of the 26 civil society organizations registered with the Civil Society Organizations Authority of Bhutan, none are registered as formal microfinance providers.[3] But some nevertheless do provide financial services. These can be referred to as the semiformal financial sector; they do not fall under specific financial sector regulation but are incorporated.

Survey responses suggest that the Bhutanese are familiar with some civil society organizations, such as the Tarayana Foundation and Loden Foundation. But few realize that some of these organizations now offer financial services. Instead, respondents associate the organizations with their social work. None of the focus group participants had obtained financial services from a civil society organization.

There is growing interest among the Bhutanese in forming cooperatives and self-help groups for saving and lending, especially in rural communities. The existing ones provide only group savings (see chapter 4), though many are considering expanding to lending services in the future.

Connecting the Disconnected · http://dx.doi.org/10.1596/978-0-8213-9834-0

Notes

1. Established in 1993, RSEBL is owned by four brokerage firms (BOB Securities Ltd., BNB Securities Ltd., Drook Securities, and RICB Securities Ltd.). Among the listed companies are five financial institutions: three banks (Druk PNB, T Bank, and BNB) and two insurance companies (RICBL and BIL).

2. See Financial Services Act of Bhutan 2011, chapter 3, on licenses and prohibitions: "11. No person shall offer financial services as a business without obtaining the appropriate license under this Act or the regulations under it; nor shall any individual fulfill a function on behalf of a financial services business without the license or registration, if any, required by this Act or the regulations under it."

3. Civil Society Organizations Authority of Bhutan, "Details of Registered CSOs," http://www.csoa.org.bt/?mode=Page&LinkID=21.

Reference

RMA (Royal Monetary Authority of Bhutan). 2012. *Annual Report 2010/11*. Thimphu: RMA.

CHAPTER 3

Financial Literacy, Financial Inclusion, and Consumer Protection

Financial literacy and consumer protection are low in Bhutan, reducing trust in the financial system. Although consumer protection regulation for financial services is being drafted, financial consumers are poorly informed about their rights, and customer service in banks does little to educate them. Efforts to extend financial inclusion will need to focus on improving financial literacy as well as customer service and access to client protection mechanisms. Otherwise, greater integration into the financial system could increase the cost of using financial products and services, especially among those who are poor or uneducated.

Financial Literacy and Management

Participants in the Bhutan Financial Inclusion Focus Group Survey did not demonstrate knowledge or practice of standard financial literacy strategies such as budgeting, cash flow management, and separate business and personal accounts. The responses suggest that the majority of Bhutanese across all economic backgrounds—including farmers, the self-employed, and salaried employees—first spend their income on food and other essentials and then pay rent, bills, and debts. They save cash left over from their purchases and bills. For example, employees who receive their salary through direct deposit in a savings account often withdraw the cash they need, leaving any surplus to accumulate as savings.

Participants in all the focus group discussions observed that they struggle to save after paying for expenses. Among farmers, savings are not only irregular but seasonal, tied to the harvest. In Thimphu people reported facing high living expenses and high levels of discretionary spending. Respondents also observed that access to ATMs has made it hard to save because the machines make it easier to withdraw money.

Despite low financial management skills, respondents identified a number of savings goals for themselves and their families. These included buying a house or land, planning for children's education, saving for retirement, and expanding their business. Respondents also compared the costs and benefits of saving money, investing it in gold, property, or land, and lending it to earn interest. Women in Thimphu pointed out that paying off a loan, investing in land, or lending money informally often offers a better return than saving in banks.[1] Other respondents preferred to save in order to achieve long-term goals such as building a house, buying a car, or opening a business.

Financial Inclusion across Demographic Groups

Though not particularly integrated into daily life, use of formal financial services is widespread in Bhutan. Compared with other South Asian countries, Bhutan performs relatively well in basic banking access. Among the survey respondents, 66 percent reported owning a savings account and 49 percent a loan account. The 2012 supply-side survey of financial institutions commissioned by the Royal Monetary Authority found a higher rate of access to savings accounts (with 80 percent of adults owning one) and a lower but nevertheless good rate of access to loan accounts (21 percent) (RMA 2012).[2] These rates compare favorably with those in the rest of the region.[3]

For Rural Communities, Constraints on Use of Financial Services

Urban Bhutanese are more integrated into the formal financial sector than rural Bhutanese are. In urban communities 80 percent of respondents reported holding a savings account, while in rural communities only 53 percent did so. Similarly, the share of rural respondents using formal loan products is almost 20 percentage points lower than the share of urban respondents doing so. The use of banking technology is dramatically lower among rural respondents: just 5 percent reported using ATMs and text message (SMS) services, compared with almost half of urban respondents. The difference in the use of financial services can be attributed to a lack of access to those services among rural populations and a lack of products tailored to their financial needs (both issues are explored further elsewhere in this book and in box 3.1).

Fieldwork suggests that rural residents have multiple sources of income. There is a growing trend of group ventures in on- and off-farm activities—such as milk associations; vegetable growers' associations; and pig, fish, and poultry farms—that can generate cash income for the farming communities. The income potential of these ventures is constrained by limited access to finance and financial services. But a significant share of the farmers interviewed reported accessing credit through BDBL's group lending scheme (see box 2.1 in chapter 2).

One rural community visited in the district of Paro benefits from the district's proximity to Thimphu: the greater mobility of people and goods in Paro supports greater financial integration. In addition, bank extension services have increased access to financial products and services in the rural communities visited. More remote regions of Bhutan are likely to have lower levels of financial inclusion than those captured in this research. Qualitative survey statistics are indicative but not nationally representative. Results from the module on access to finance

Box 3.1 Accessing Financial Services Often Difficult and Costly in Rural Bhutanese Communities

In the district of Samtse there are 17 village clusters (*chiwogs*), among which Lamjee is the most remote. There are no roads to Lamjee. Indeed, people need to walk six hours from the village just to reach the nearest farm road. From there it takes another two hours to walk the 4 kilometers to the municipal center of Hathkhola. Few vehicles travel this road, and a taxi would cost about Nu 500 (US$9.00) round-trip. The nearest bank is in the town of Samtse, another 12 kilometers down the road from Hathkhola. Taxi fare for this leg is usually Nu 100 (US$1.80) round-trip, though when transport is in high demand the cost can increase to Nu 400 (US$7.20). Reaching Samtse from Lamjee in one day is practically impossible, so people often spend the night on the road. They may stay with someone they know or pay for lodging. In total, it can take eight and half hours and up to Nu 1,100 (US$19.80) to reach the nearest bank from Lamjee. The minimum estimated cost is Nu 300 (US$5.40) if most of the journey is done on foot.

Assuming that a client from Lamjee requests the smallest loan that BDBL offers, Nu 5,000 (US$90), the transportation costs would amount to 6–22 percent of the loan. Moreover, loans are rarely approved on a client's first visit, so the client could spend half the loan on transportation to and from the bank. Another 44 percent could be added for the estimated opportunity cost of lost work on the client's farm. Other costs include legal stamps, photocopies, legal fees, and expenses arising from any delay.

Lamjee is particularly remote. But this example nevertheless illustrates the challenges of extending financial access in remote regions of Bhutan.

Source: Bhutan Financial Inclusion Focus Group Survey 2012.

in the Bhutan Living Standard Survey 2012 will provide nationwide quantitative data on the use of formal financial services by Bhutanese households (see NSB forthcoming).

With Wealth and Connections, Greater Financial Inclusion

There is significant disparity in financial inclusion among economic groups. Unsurprisingly, entrepreneurs and business owners are the most financially integrated of the groups interviewed. Among the business owners interviewed, all reported owning a savings account, and more than half use ATMs and SMS services; Internet banking is less useful for them. By contrast, among the farmers interviewed, 25 percent reported not having a bank account, and responses from those who do have a savings account suggested that they rarely use it. Farmers have taken out loans just as often as entrepreneurs, though almost all were group loans granted by BDBL.

Respondents observed that economic status can be more important than type of employment when seeking a loan. Because financial institutions require collateral, wealthy individuals with land and buildings are better able to obtain financing. Poor respondents reported greater difficulty in obtaining credit because of lack of collateral.

Connecting the Disconnected • http://dx.doi.org/10.1596/978-0-8213-9834-0

Women Knowledgeable about Financial Services but Could Be Further Targeted

Female respondents' rate of integration into the formal financial system is similar to that of their male counterparts, but women also expressed significant knowledge about formal financial services. Just as among their male counterparts, urban women tend to be more financially integrated than rural women and more comfortable taking on new financial products and services. Just over half of female respondents use a formal savings or loan product, though they also keep additional savings in expensive clothes, coral, jewelry, and gold ornaments as well as in savings schemes for their children's education (see discussion in chapter 4 on investment as a savings strategy). Men are more inclined to invest in land, a house, a vehicle, or business expansion—investments that often require a loan. These results need further corroboration, since the survey results do not make it possible to determine whether female respondents attributed household accounts (accounts that may have been opened by their husband) as their own.

The role of women in Bhutan suggests that they may be an appropriate target for efforts to increase use of formal financial services. Financial inclusion among women in Bhutan is high relative to that in regional neighbors, but the importance of their role in society suggests that it could be even higher. In Bhutan, in contrast with the rest of South Asia, inheritance rights and land and property rights have traditionally been vested in women (see Pain and Pema 2004)—though women who were interviewed did not share personal experiences in leveraging land for a loan.

In addition, rural women are increasingly responsible for bringing farm produce to market and managing household finances. It was reported that men dedicate their time to labor while women take charge of financial management, including banking services, in addition to participating in farm labor. As a result, particularly in rural areas, women appeared to be well informed and knowledgeable about financial products. Nevertheless, the share of rural women who reported using formal financial services is smaller than the share of rural entrepreneurs or farmers—male and female—who reported doing so.

Finally, field research found that women feel more comfortable than men in managing banking technology such as ATMs and mobile phone banking. Their higher comfort levels suggest that they would be an appropriate market segment for targeting technology services.

All these factors—women's landownership, their role in marketing the products of family businesses, and their expressed interest in banking technology—suggest a potential for women to be more integrated into the formal financial system than the research findings describe. Indeed, women may be an untapped market segment for greater use of formal financial services.

For Youth, a Link between Employment and Financial Access

Among the four respondent groups, young adults (ages 18–24) are the least financially integrated. Because young people are still studying and investing in their development, they are the least inclined to save. Just a quarter of respondents in this group reported having opened a savings account. Because many young adults do not work and rely on their families for support, they fall out of the target client group for financial institutions. For example, two young participants from Paro reported that they had tried to get education loans but their applications were denied because they had no collateral. Young participants from Mongar and Thimphu said that it would help them if collateral-free loans could be made available for small entrepreneurial activities. Youth need employment to gain financial access, but financial access could help them gain employment.

Young people also tend to self-exclude from financial products and services. Young respondents from Thimphu expressed hesitancy about approaching banks because of their lack of experience. One participant said, "It helps if you know someone in the bank or when there is a friend to go with you … You are lost and there are so many people and counters. Everyone looks so busy, and it is daunting to even go there." Young participants also said that they are not taken seriously by financial institutions and prefer not to interact with the formal financial sector.

Consumer Protection

More effective financial consumer protection is a clear need in Bhutan, with separate regulation yet to be issued in this area and currently no systematic efforts by financial service providers to educate clients about their rights. As an additional client protection measure, financial service providers also need to take due care not to overexpose clients while extending credit.

A Need for Consumer Protection Regulation

No regulation on financial consumer protection exists in Bhutan, although the Companies Act 2000 and Consumer Protection Act of Bhutan 2012 broadly address some consumer protection rights.[4] A key measure in providing consumer protection is to establish affordable, independent, fair, accountable, and timely mechanisms and processes for redress of grievances. Fieldwork provided a number of examples in which financial consumers received improper treatment and had little or no recourse. Respondents were often unaware of mechanisms for submitting complaints about treatment or services received in the financial sector or found them to be inadequate (box 3.2). People uninformed about their rights with respect to financial institutions or unaware of opportunities to claim redress are less likely to defend themselves. Poor and uneducated consumers may be especially likely to fall into this group.

Customer Service Culture Lacking among Banks

Customers of financial institutions in Bhutan are poorly informed about their rights and responsibilities, in part because of the lack of a customer service culture among banks. Many respondents reported feeling intimidated when visiting a bank because cashiers and loan officers work quickly to finish with each customer so as to attend to the long lines behind them. Customers often do not have enough time to absorb the complicated financial paperwork in front of them. In addition, most bank documents are in English, which most rural and elderly people do not speak, read, or write.

Box 3.2 Some Focus Group Findings on Failed Consumer Protection Mechanisms in Bhutan

Focus group discussions turned up several examples of participants encountering problems with consumer protection mechanisms. One woman reported paying an additional Nu 65,000 (US$1,170) on a loan that had already been repaid and for which the bank had issued a clearance letter. She is appealing the fee in court but finds the process costly and time consuming. Another reported paying an extra Nu 27,000 (US$486) because of the negligence of bank staff. She almost filed a case in court but decided against it because of the costs she would incur in loss of time working her farm and in travel and legal expenses. She concluded that the cost of appealing was greater than the amount owed to her.

Other participants reported finding discrepancies between their payments and the amount their bank deducted from their loan amount. One participant explained that banks often charge clients for late payments when computer systems fail and the banks are unable to accept deposits. Respondents also felt that legal documents contain little protection for the consumer and always benefit the bank; nevertheless, they felt pressured to sign the documents to get the loan.

Source: Bhutan Financial Inclusion Focus Group Survey 2012.

Equitable and fair treatment is a core indicator of consumer protection. In all the survey locations respondents raised concerns about treatment by bank staff.[5] Other participants pointed out that obtaining a loan often depends on one's relationship with bank staff. "Banks have double standards and not all clients are treated equally," said one respondent. Another commented that "if you are an uneducated person, even the security guard at the door starts mistreating you."

While some of these perceptions may be linked to issues of financial literacy, they also highlight the need for customer service standards in the financial sector. Efforts to extend financial inclusion will need to incorporate a financial literacy component as well as improvements in customer service and increased access to client protection mechanisms. Without such measures, greater integration into the financial system could increase the cost of using financial products and services, especially among poor or uneducated people.

Information on Client Indebtedness Limited

Part of consumer protection is to ensure that lending practices do not overexpose financial consumers to debt. Credit scoring and credit histories help in this, but they are not widely used in Bhutan. Moreover, the survey found little awareness of issues linked to overindebtedness among focus group participants. The lack of awareness suggests that the Bhutanese are not well informed about what overindebtedness means or what its financial implications are.

The Credit Information Bureau aims to protect against overindebtedness by consolidating credit information from member institutions to develop individual credit reports. But informal loans are not reported to the credit bureau, reducing the value of the individual credit reports. The example of one respondent illustrates the challenges of capturing credit information: The respondent borrowed Nu 50,000 (US$900) from a moneylender for an annual community religious ceremony (*puja*). When she was unable to repay the loan on time, she borrowed money from her father-in-law to pay the moneylender. She later took out an education loan of Nu 150,000 (US$2,700) to repay her father-in-law. The widespread use of informal lending makes it difficult for bank risk divisions to evaluate potential credit clients.

Training in providing credit scoring and credit histories would help banks identify clients who are overindebted or represent higher credit risks. In addition, credit scoring would allow banks to introduce more modern lending techniques for clients who cannot meet collateral requirements.

Notes

1. The highest interest rate for savings in a fixed deposit for five years is 8.5 percent a year in most banks in Bhutan (with the account subject to restrictions on withdrawals and deposits), while the lowest loan interest rate that people pay to banks is 10 percent a year. As reported in the survey, if people lend money informally, it will earn a minimum of 2–10 percent a month in interest.

2. A presentation of the supply-side survey results nonetheless indicated that the share of adults with an individual savings account is in reality lower because the number of savings accounts reflected in the results likely includes accounts used for businesses though registered as individual accounts (see RMA 2012).

3. According to 2011 data from the World Bank's Global Financial Inclusion (Global Findex) Database, access in South Asia ranges from 69 percent of adults having a bank account and 18 percent a bank loan in Sri Lanka to 9 percent having a bank account and 7 percent a bank loan in Afghanistan.

4. Other acts address financial consumer protection through increased competition and an enabling policy and regulatory environment in the financial sector, including the RMA Act 2010 (repealing RMA Act 1982), Prudential Regulations 2002, Financial Services Act of Bhutan 2011, Corporate Governance Regulations 2011, and Movable and Immovable Property Act of the Kingdom of Bhutan 1999.

5. For example, one woman said that she was denied credit while her friend's application was approved, and the bank did not explain the reason for the rejection.

References

Global Financial Inclusion (Global Findex) Database. World Bank, Washington, DC.

NSB (National Statistics Bureau). Forthcoming. *Bhutan Living Standard Survey 2012 Report*. Thimphu: NSB.

Pain, A., and D. Pema. 2004. "The Matrilineal Inheritance of Land in Bhutan." *Contemporary South Asia* 13 (4): 421–35.

RMA (Royal Monetary Authority of Bhutan). 2012. "Supply-Side Access to Finance: Key Findings." Paper presented at a meeting of the Financial Inclusion Policy Working Group, Thimphu, April.

CHAPTER 4

Formal and Informal Savings Strategies

Participants in the Bhutan Financial Inclusion Focus Group Survey reported saving both at home and in banks, with home-based savings functioning much as a checking account does. Savings kept in banks are often designated for larger purchases or long-term savings goals. Since cash at home generally goes toward short-term or lower-value savings goals, respondents keep smaller amounts at home than in banks. But this does not take into account the investment of savings in property, jewelry, or durable goods, which appears to be a common practice in Bhutan. The practice of in-kind saving makes it more difficult to value respondents' total savings.

What People Save For

Survey respondents shared a number of savings goals, though as discussed in chapter 3 most do not use basic financial management strategies that could help them achieve those goals. Short-term savings goals include covering food purchases, school expenses for children, and emergencies such as illness, death, and other unforeseen social expenses. People from the farming community in Thimphu save money to pay laborers who work on their farm.[1] Long-term savings goals include purchasing land, constructing a house, expanding a business, paying for children's education, and coping with natural disasters. Respondents frequently mentioned saving for religious ceremonies, festivals, and pilgrimages along with life events such as childbirth, weddings, retirement, and death.

Where People Save

Savings accounts are the most popular and widely used financial service in Bhutan. But they remain inconvenient and unresponsive to the need to make small, infrequent deposits. While two-thirds of respondents own a savings account, their use of the account varies greatly. Some people, especially entrepreneurs, make deposits and withdrawals daily or weekly, while others reported using their account infrequently or hardly at all. Savings accounts are used mostly for long-term savings; checking accounts appear to be less frequently used. People rarely reported saving with informal lenders or informal institutions.

Varied Strategies for Home-Based Saving

People in all the survey locations save informally at home, often in addition to using a formal savings account. They often keep short-term savings in cash at home, since these funds are more liquid and convenient than those kept in a bank. They keep long-term savings either in a bank or at home, though as the amount saved increases, respondents are more likely to own a savings account. Most rural people save at home rather than in banks because they have very small and frequent needs and traveling to the city to withdraw money from banks is inconvenient. Even in Thimphu's peripheral communities people save at home when their income is small or infrequent.

Home-based savings strategies are varied: people save cash, they purchase durable goods, and they invest in property. Cash is mostly stored in boxes, in cupboards, or between clothes. Women are more likely to save in kind by purchasing expensive *kira* (traditional dresses worn by women in Bhutan), coral, jewelry, gold ornaments, household items, or livestock. Respondents viewed savings in the form of *kira* and jewelry as semiliquid assets that could be converted into cash in an emergency. Such assets are preferable to cash, especially for people who fear that they would spend the cash. Savers in rural areas invest in livestock, improved seeds, farm improvement, farming equipment, and other farm inputs.

Storing savings in goods rather than in a bank has potential drawbacks. The amount people receive from the sale of such goods could vary, and it is possible that others will take advantage of someone selling their possessions in an emergency. In addition, people are less informed about the total savings they have and less able to leverage those savings for investments.

Preferences in Saving in Banks

Making small, regular savings deposits in banks is not common practice. Barriers to more frequent account use include distance to a bank and costs associated with getting there and waiting in line. Another is a belief that depositing small amounts is embarrassing, indicative of one's poverty. People worry about what bank cashiers might say or think. Participants from Mongar and Paro revealed that they are embarrassed to approach banks for small deposits even though banks accept a minimum deposit of Nu 50 (US$0.90). Unless they have Nu 500 (US$9) or more to deposit, they save money at home rather than in a bank. Preferences are similar in urban areas: women in Thimphu find making small, regular deposits tedious. They reported that they would make deposits in a formal bank only in amounts of Nu 5,000 (US$90) or more.

People's choice of banks is limited, and is often determined by accessibility, the need for a certain product or service, or their employer's preference for making direct deposits. Bhutan Development Bank Limited (BDBL), as the only bank operating in rural areas, is the formal savings option for many respondents.

Respondents with children studying in India use Druk Punjab National Bank Limited (PNB) because it offers remittance services and an ATM card that their children can use abroad. Government employees have savings accounts with Bank of Bhutan Limited (BOB) because they are required to provide a BOB account for direct deposit of their salary. Corporate and private sector workers in urban areas reported saving with a greater variety of banks, though they frequently mentioned Bhutan National Bank Limited (BNB) and BOB.

Emergence of Group Savings Schemes

Group savings schemes and cooperatives are slowly emerging in Bhutan in response to the demand for saving locally and in small amounts. Some people in rural regions save through group savings schemes or recurrent deposits of Nu 500 (US$9) and below. Savings clubs are run by community members who understand and respect the savings capacity of contributors.[2] Respondents considered making contributions to savings clubs faster and more convenient than making deposits in banks.

There is an opportunity for savings clubs and cooperatives to serve as a stepping-stone for rural communities until financial infrastructure or innovations in technology help integrate households into the formal financial system. In the meantime, support and capacity building for club management will be critical to ensure that people's savings are protected. Successful savings groups in Niger and Zanzibar, based on models widely replicated in other economies, illustrate the potential role of community-driven programs in meeting the financial needs of poor people (see appendix F).

Investment as a Savings and Income-Generating Strategy

In addition to saving at home or in a bank, many respondents reported investing their savings. Investments in real estate, businesses, or informal lending can bring a higher rate of return than savings in a bank account. People reported investing savings in land, in the construction of a house, in a vehicle, in business expansion, in farm improvements, or in education. Men tend to direct more savings into investments than women do, though this difference may reflect their ability to earn more money. Savings that are intended for an investment are generally kept in a bank.

Investments in housing have always been popular, driven by the dream of buying a plot of land to build a home. Recent increases in housing construction are also due to the shortage of housing and high demand for rental housing stemming from migration to urban areas and the 2011 earthquake. In communities near Thimphu, where there is high rental demand, housing construction is a popular form of investment because rentals bring a steady income. One respondent observed that "Dhazhi community is on the outskirts of Thimphu city, where there is high demand for housing and therefore people build houses on the farmland instead of cultivating it." Another participant added that building a house is rewarding because it means that people "don't have to work in the sun and rain" but can instead collect rental income every month.

People also invest in education schemes, savings schemes offered by financial institutions to allow parents to provide for their children's higher education. Respondents reported that colleges have become very expensive and competitive. Parents want to ensure that even if they are struck by some misfortune, they have at least secured their children's education. Since admission to government colleges is limited, parents save or invest in education schemes to ensure that they can pay for a private college education if their children do not qualify for fully funded government colleges.

Notes

1. Historically laborers were paid in kind with food or other goods, but today farmers must pay laborers in cash at the end of the day.
2. Informal cooperatives and groups are known as *tshogpas* or *deytshen* (for example, people generally call a dairy cooperative a *gonor tshogpa* or *gonor deytshen*) and savings groups as *sojog ma nguel deytshen*.

CHAPTER 5

Formal and Informal Lending

Formal lending services in Bhutan are limited and directed to the few people who own property that can be used as collateral. Banks' strict collateral requirements and long loan processing times encourage people to turn to the informal sector, where loan approvals are based more on trust and personal relationships. Participants in the Bhutan Financial Inclusion Focus Group Survey voiced concern that banks undervalue collateral and thus underfinance the investment associated with a loan, increasing the risk that the borrower will be unable to repay it. Informal lenders—who might seem riskier to outside observers—were seen as preferable because of a perception that borrowers have more rights with respect to these lenders.

Typical Loan Amounts across Areas and Sectors

Compared with loans reported by people in rural communities, those reported by people in urban and economically vibrant areas were typically larger, suggesting that borrowers in these areas have greater opportunities to access large financing. In urban and economically vibrant Thimphu the smallest formal loan reported was for Nu 7,500 (US$135), while the largest was for Nu 1.5 million (US$27,000) (except for an extreme outlier reported by one respondent, a construction loan for Nu 20 million, or US$360,000). Both loans were for the construction of a house. By contrast, the largest loan reported by respondents in urban and less economically vibrant Mongar was for Nu 800,000 (US$14,400), for education. In rural and poor Samtse the largest was a business loan amounting to Nu 90,000 (US$1,620).

The pattern is similar for informal loans. The largest amount reported to have been borrowed from a moneylender was Nu 3 million (US$54,000), by a Thimphu respondent. The loan was taken as a bridge loan for a business because the bank loan, though approved, was not ready. Across other survey sites, the largest amounts participants reported borrowing from the informal sector were Nu 1.5 million (US$27,000) in rural but more economically vibrant Paro, Nu 500,000 (US$9,000) in Mongar, and Nu 50,000 (US$900) in Samtse.

Connecting the Disconnected • http://dx.doi.org/10.1596/978-0-8213-9834-0

The terms and conditions for formal and informal loans differ substantially (see appendix G). Formal loans are based on fixed assets collateral and involve large investments of time and resources to fulfill the processing requirements. By contrast, informal loans can be obtained quickly and on the basis of a relationship rather than collateral. While formal loans are restricted to borrowers who have assets that can be used as collateral, they also tend to be less costly. Formal lenders may charge interest of 10–15 percent a year, while informal lenders tend to charge 2–10 percent a month. Despite the higher interest rates, the ease of obtaining an informal loan increased respondents' preference for informal lenders.

Formal Lending

Formal lending in Bhutan is not inclusive: most of the formal credit goes to only a small percentage of the population. Even though credit growth has been strong in the past 10 years, access to credit remains constrained for the majority of the population (box 5.1). Borrowers who do obtain formal loans use them primarily for housing construction; this was the most common use for bank loans reported across all survey sites and also accounted for the largest loans. People also seek loans to buy land, property, or vehicles; to expand their business or improve their farm; to finance their children's education; or to pay for emergencies, religious celebrations, or gambling debts. Banks finance larger loans and loans for housing, property, and education, while informal lenders fill in the gaps by offering smaller amounts and loans for expenses that banks will not finance.

Respondents reported that the type of collateral required for a bank loan limits opportunities for obtaining formal credit. Most banks require commercial assets as collateral; in rural areas only BDBL accepts clients' land or home as collateral. In addition, many respondents believe that banks' property valuation for collateral is too low and that banks offer loans based on a percentage of their low valuation, reducing the size of the loan a client can obtain. Respondents perceived the loan amounts for which they were approved as too small to successfully make the investment they proposed, reducing their ability to repay the loan.

The wide use of *collateral-based lending* may stem in part from poor business practices and constraints on banks' ability to roll out cash-flow-based lending. Urban participants, including business owners, often observed that bank staff are not equipped to carry out proper project feasibility studies to assess loan risk and that as a result banks require high collateral coverage to minimize the financial risks. But part of the explanation may be weaknesses in record keeping. The survey team observed that business owners who were interviewed tend to keep poor records of their sales and cash flow, limiting the information that banks can obtain about the strength of the business. In addition, the geographic distances between banks and businesses make it difficult for loan officers to carry out a feasibility study of a project. Without clear indications of the viability of a business or project and the likelihood that a loan can be repaid, banks resort to collateral-based lending to hedge their risk.

Box 5.1 Financial Inclusion Still a Challenge in Bhutan despite Sustained Credit Growth

Credit to the private sector has increased rapidly in Bhutan. While Bhutan's robust economic growth partially explains this increase, credit to the private sector as a percentage of GDP has also risen sharply, more than doubling since 2007 (figure B5.1.1). Also playing a role is the entry of the two new private commercial banks, which have brought greater competition into the banking system and have accounted for roughly a third of the recent growth in credit.

But the credit growth has been concentrated in only a few sectors. In 2010 the expansion of credit was directed mainly to the building and construction sector and the transport sector. In 2011 personal loans also increased, together with credit to manufacturing, trade and commerce, and construction (figure B5.1.2). Notably left behind has been the agricultural sector, with loans amounting to less than 2 percent of the total loan portfolio of the financial sector (RMA 2012).

Also overlooked are rural areas, even though they are home to the majority of the population. Rural areas are also poorer and more financially constrained than urban areas (75 percent of the country's poor people live in rural areas, most of them daily wage earners, self-employed householders, or landless laborers). This gap between rural and urban areas

Figure B5.1.1 Bank Credit to the Private Sector in Bhutan, 2000–11

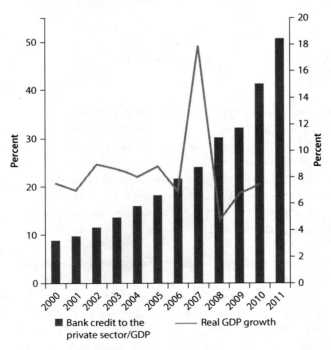

■ Bank credit to the private sector/GDP ——— Real GDP growth

Sources: For bank credit, International Monetary Fund, International Financial Statistics database; for GDP growth, World Bank, World Development Indicators database.
Note: GDP = gross domestic product.

box continues next page

Box 5.1 Financial Inclusion Still a Challenge in Bhutan despite Sustained Credit Growth *(continued)*

Figure B5.1.2 Sectoral Decomposition of Bank Credit to the Private Sector in Bhutan, 2007–11

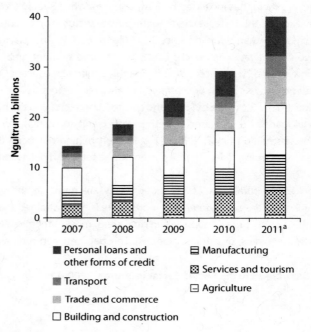

Source: Royal Monetary Authority of Bhutan.
a. Data refer to the period January through June.

stems in large part from Bhutan's mountainous geography and low population density, which have made physical access to remote rural areas a challenge (for more on rural-urban disparities, see chapter 3). To be consistent with Bhutan's vision for peace, prosperity, and happiness (see Gross National Happiness Commission 1999), it is essential to ensure that the poor, the vulnerable, and the marginalized segments of its population are included in financial sector development as well as in the overall development process. Ensuring that these groups are brought into the mainstream of the economy and society could also contribute to increasing domestic production and in turn help to contain the growing current account deficits with India.

How widespread is the use of formal credit among the Bhutanese population? Based on supply-side data from financial institutions, the Royal Monetary Authority estimates that just 21 percent of adults have a loan account, though this figure is probably an overestimate because some people may hold more than one loan account (RMA 2012). The qualitative survey found that half of respondents have had a loan from a formal financial institution at one time in their life. This share may be slightly higher than that in the overall population, however, because the survey did not reach the most marginalized communities.

The complex and time-consuming procedures entailed in obtaining formal financing act as a disincentive for many potential borrowers. Once a client has submitted the necessary documents, it takes a month or more for the loan to be approved. The longest processing time reported by a respondent was three months, for a housing loan. Processing times for group loans are shorter, and loans for less than Nu 50,000 (US$900) can be obtained in a week.

Respondents perceive all banks as providing similar products and services, so people choose a provider on the basis of customer service, relationships with bank staff, and convenience. Relationships with staff appear to be an important factor in getting approved for a loan as well as in choosing a lender. Participants in both urban and rural communities said that when seeking a loan, they usually approach a bank where someone they know works, since that often makes getting a loan faster and easier.

Informal Lending

Informal loans are widely used in Bhutan, covering a variety of needs that formal financing does not meet. Among the range of those providing informal financing are relatives, moneylenders, and religious institutions.

The Wide Reach of Informal Lending

Informal lending has a wide reach in rural and urban areas, often operating alongside formal lending. Informal loans are used by households that have relationships with formal financial institutions as well as by those that do not. Businesspeople in urban areas borrow from moneylenders when they lack sufficient collateral for investments they wish to make.

Family members and friends are the most common and preferred source of informal loans because they charge little or no interest. But they may have limited lending capacity. Loans from family members are typically used for small, urgent expenses such as school uniforms or fees, doctors' fees, and other social expenses. If unable to borrow from a family member, people will often seek a loan from someone they know or from a moneylender.

Moneylenders tend to be more active in rural areas and among poor households, but the poorest households seem to rely on family and friends. As noted in chapter 2, moneylenders are typically wealthier community members—though that description can encompass a wide range of individuals and even institutions. In rural areas both the lender and the borrower are usually from the same community, though in some instances moneylenders offer loans to people they do not know. Because moneylenders often live in the same community or area as those who borrow from them, informal lending offers the advantage of less time and cost for travel.

How Informal Lending Compares with Formal Lending

Informal loans appear to fall into two categories: those that replicate formal loan products and those that finance activities not covered by formal institutions.

Activities that may not be approved for a formal loan include religious ceremonies (*pujas*), weddings or dowries, pilgrimages, payments on other debts, gambling, and emergencies such as illness, death, or natural disasters. Farmers often use informal loan products because banks do not offer seasonal loans, which are repaid at the end of the harvest. And entrepreneurs often seek bridge loans from informal lenders as an interim measure when formal loan approvals take too long, paying off the moneylender once the bank loan is disbursed.

The informal lending sector is viewed as more competitive than the formal sector because it offers products and services better suited to the needs of low-income households—with fewer procedures, less paperwork, and faster approvals than for formal loans. Formal financial institutions are unable to provide small, quick loans because of the constraints of distance, cost, and time. Informal lending, often relationship based and characterized by little paperwork, fills in the gaps. Survey participants mentioned that moneylenders may bypass a written contract if the amount borrowed is small (less than Nu 30,000, or US$540) and the borrower is a reliable person with a good borrowing record with the lender. Informal lenders typically do not require collateral, since loans are based on the lender's knowledge of and trust in the client.

Respondents viewed informal loans as better tailored to the economic realities of typical customers. For example, respondents felt that bank loans were not tailored to the needs of farmers, who often need financing to purchase seed and fertilizer at the beginning of the growing season but cannot pay off the loan until the harvest. Banks often require farmers to begin paying their loan the month after it is processed, while informal lenders will defer payments until the end of the season. In addition, informal lenders are more willing than banks to consider lending to poor people, though informal loans are often significantly smaller. Banks are willing to give loans to finance children's education only to those with a salaried job or plenty of assets, effectively excluding poor families who may wish to invest in their children's education to improve their well-being. Recent innovations such as BDBL's launch of mobile banks in rural areas are viewed favorably, but inconsistent implementation has reduced their impact. Efforts to extend financial inclusion need to consider the value that informal lenders offer and find ways to profitably replicate their services within formal financial institutions.

While informal loans are perceived as better suited to the needs of many, they can also involve higher costs for borrowers because lenders hedge their risks with higher interest rates. To operate legally in Bhutan, lenders need a license and must pay taxes, but many informal lenders do not fulfill these obligations. In addition, informal lenders might charge as much as 15 percent interest a month, though by law lenders cannot charge more than 15 percent a year.[1] Respondents reported that moneylenders often add interest charges exceeding 15 percent a year to the capital in a loan agreement so that they can petition for the full amount in court if the borrower defaults. One woman who was taken to court for defaulting on an informal loan reported that the lender threatened her to prevent her from disclosing the 10 percent monthly interest he had charged.

After more than a year in court she paid Nu 32,000 (US$576) more than she had originally contracted for.

In rural areas some respondents reported contracting with informal lenders to repay debts through farm labor; their loan payments would be automatically deducted from their wages. No respondents shared concerns about their safety in dealing with informal lenders. Even so, the threat of bonded labor and the considerable power moneylenders hold in the community suggest that informal lending can undermine borrowers' personal well-being as well as their financial well-being.

Moreover, informal lending increases risks of overindebtedness—especially for borrowers who use a mix of formal and informal lending services. Reliance on informal lenders also increases the risk of overindebtedness because informal lenders base lending decisions more on trust and social connections than on careful analysis of a client's ability to repay the loan. In Mongar the municipal government reported that defaults on informal loans result in five to six court cases a year.

Role of Religious Institutions

Religious institutions are an important source of informal loans. They are by far the oldest and most established institutions in the country, and people make offerings in cash and in kind to demonstrate their faith and devotion. These contributions provide capital that allows institutions such as senior monks (*dragays*), lay monks (*gomchens*), and temples (*lhakhangs*) to provide loans to members of the community. Religious institutions charge lower interest rates than other informal lenders, around 2 percent a month. Borrowers may include anyone from the community or the social circle. While religious institutions place few restrictions on lending, they are unlikely to offer a loan intended for pig, fish, or poultry farming, since such practices conflict with their religious principles.

While lending by religious institutions may not have a profit motive, it may contribute to overindebtedness, particularly because the loans are not reported to the Credit Information Bureau. One woman reported borrowing Nu 700,000 (US$12,600) from a religious institution. When she was ready to pay it back, the institution requested that she keep the capital and continue to pay the interest, which was used to finance an annual religious ceremony (*puja*) in the community. Researcher Karma Galay (2001) describes how people in the community of Chapcha pay additional interest on loans from their local monastery (*goenpa*) as their contribution to the institution. While overpayments of debt to religious institutions may be considered devotional obligations, they also mean higher costs for financial services.

Note

1. Section 17 of the Movable and Immovable Property Act of the Kingdom of Bhutan 1999.

Connecting the Disconnected · http://dx.doi.org/10.1596/978-0-8213-9834-0

References

Galay, K. 2001. "Bhutanese Context of Civil Society." *Journal of Bhutan Studies* 3 (1): 199–218.

Gross National Happiness Commission. 1999. *Bhutan 2020: A Vision for Peace, Prosperity and Happiness.* Thimphu: Gross National Happiness Commission.

RMA (Royal Monetary Authority of Bhutan). 2012. "Supply-Side Access to Finance: Key Findings." Paper presented at a meeting of the Financial Inclusion Policy Working Group, Thimphu, April.

CHAPTER 6

Remittances, Insurance, and Technology

Remittances, insurance, and technology are all potential tools for extending financial inclusion in Bhutan. Financial institutions offering products and services linked to remittances could potentially attract nontraditional bank users, though the nature of migration and remittances in Bhutan has not yet created opportunities for doing so. The Bhutan Financial Inclusion Focus Group Survey found that there is great interest in insurance products but little understanding of them, with few people aware of the types of insurance available. Tailoring insurance products to people's needs could potentially extend financial access to nontraditional users. Technology in financial services is another tool that policy makers hope can increase interest in and use of formal financial services. But despite good mobile infrastructure across Bhutan, the mobile phone banking services available in the country respond to the financial needs of only a small share of the population.

Remittance Patterns and Services

Outflows dominate in Bhutan's international remittances. Formal outflows amounted to 4.2 percent of GDP in 2010. Official international inflows remain small, though data show a steady increase between 2006 and 2010 to US$5.66 million—equivalent to 0.33 percent of GDP (World Bank 2011). Survey respondents reported using international remittance services to send money to children studying in India, though a few also use these services to make international business payments or to receive money from family members abroad.

Domestic remittance services are used for sending or receiving business payments or salaries or for transfers between family members (such as for consumption, housing construction, education, and pilgrimages). Field research found that informal flows remain dominant in domestic remittances between migrants and their family or friends within Bhutan. Informal remittances tend to be smaller and are sent with bus or taxi drivers and travelers. Family, friends, and neighbors may not charge for their help in delivering a remittance, but bus and taxi drivers charge between Nu 50 and Nu 200 (US$0.90–4.00) per transfer. One respondent who owns a taxi justified his rate by citing the time he spends looking for the recipient of the remittance and the risk he takes in handling the money.

Among formal providers of remittance services, commercial banks and Bhutan Post are the largest. Money transfer operators operate only through Bhutan Post (in the case of Western Union) and Bhutan National Bank Limited (BNB) (MoneyGram). All other banks in Bhutan also provide remittance services. Convenience, cost, efficiency, safety, and speed were the most important characteristics respondents cited for choosing a remittance service provider, though people also tend to use the same bank for remittances as they use for saving and borrowing. BNB, Bank of Bhutan Limited (BOB), and Bhutan Development Bank Limited (BDBL) offer free account-to-account transfers within the same bank and charge Nu 20–40 (US$0.36–0.72) for transfers between banks. Respondents who have children studying in India tend to use Druk Punjab National Bank Limited (Druk PNB), a joint venture of India's Punjab National Bank and local promoters, because it is cheaper and more convenient; the bank does not charge fees for remittances under Nu 30,000 (US$540) to India's Punjab National Bank. In areas where Druk PNB does not offer remittance services, respondents use BOB, BNB, and Western Union. Some respondents reported using Western Union because it is fast and safe but to a lesser extent than other service providers because it is also more expensive.

In urban areas people more frequently use formal remittance channels because they are safe and convenient. Rural residents resort to informal channels because formal providers are too far away and because these providers often use forms that are in English, which most rural residents are not comfortable with.

Knowledge and Use of Insurance Services

In Bhutan use of insurance is limited mostly to home and life insurance, which households are required to purchase. In addition, financial institutions require borrowers to insure their collateralized assets. For these reasons many respondents were able to identify one or more insurance policies that they hold, including home, life, vehicle, machinery, livestock, and education insurance. Just five respondents voluntarily hold insurance policies. And a local leader in the community surveyed in Paro observed that only 30 households out of 560 have fire insurance.

While respondents could identify their insurance policies, they were often uninformed about the details of the policies. Research found that respondents did not know details about their policy's coverage, the claims process, and sometimes even the provider. And there was little understanding of the nationally required home and life insurance. Since the premiums are paid along with taxes, most believe that the insurance is a government service, though policies are offered by Royal Insurance Corporation of Bhutan Limited (RICBL) or the private insurance company Bhutan Insurance Limited (BIL).[1] The 2011 earthquake renewed interest in comprehensive home insurance policies, because the few households that held a comprehensive policy received compensation. Others were disappointed to learn that their policies covered fire but not earthquake damage. Perhaps because of the poor understanding of insurance policies, respondents expressed frustration with making claims. They found the process time consuming and fraught with delays.

The limited uptake of insurance appears to be linked to the poor understanding of the types of insurance available, including health, livestock, and travel insurance. One respondent observed that people in his community would like to insure their cattle and crops, but he believed that no such policies existed. When he learned that agricultural insurance did exist, he commented that it would probably require monthly payments; in fact, the premium could be paid once a year, during the harvest. If more people understood insurance products, there would probably be greater demand for a tool that protects well-being during times of hardship.

Use and Potential of Technology in Financial Services

Access to bank branches is limited in the rural and remote areas of Bhutan. According to 2011 data, the country has only about 2.2 commercial bank branches and 1.9 ATMs per 1,000 square kilometers, compared with an average in South Asia of 36.44 branches and 32.96 ATMs per 1,000 square kilometers.[2] In addition, ATMs, credit cards, and Internet banking are mostly available only in urban areas, where the infrastructure exists to support them. By contrast, mobile phones have made significant inroads into rural areas. Even so, low English-language literacy and lack of familiarity reduce the interest in using the modern technologies that are available for financial services. Financial innovation could potentially trigger improvements in access in remote parts of Bhutan.

Respondents reported using ATMs to withdraw cash and make balance inquiries. Banks offer a deposit service through ATMs as well, but no one reported using this service, probably because it accepts only checks and not cash. People may also prefer to receive a deposit slip from the service counter. The 26 percent of respondents who use ATMs consider them convenient for withdrawing cash and helpful because they make it possible to keep less cash on hand. Respondents would like to see more ATMs installed and better backup systems in place to increase their reliability.

Mobile phones are widespread in Bhutan, but mobile phone banking is not.[3] In Thimphu a few respondents use mobile phone banking to receive messages about account balances and advertisements. In other communities almost all respondents expressed difficulty in reading the English-language letters and numbers on mobile phones. Since few understand English letters and numbers, they get help from friends or family to make a call, or memorize the buttons they need to press to call their contacts. Familiarity with mobile phone technology is a major hurdle in achieving widespread use of mobile phone banking, and the predominance of English in this banking technology will continue to inhibit uptake even as mobile phones become more integrated into daily life.

Distrust in and unfamiliarity with mobile phone banking services are also deterrents to adopting this technology. Because people use the technology infrequently, they feel uncertain about their ability to use it correctly, worrying that they might press the wrong button and transfer their savings into someone else's account.

Interestingly, a large share of female respondents—almost half, compared with a quarter of all focus group participants—reported using ATMs or mobile phone banking. Their use rate is close to that among entrepreneurs. All the women who reported using these services live in urban areas. As with other financial services, women's apparent comfort with ATMs and mobile phone banking represents an opportunity to extend financial services to them and their families.

Internet banking services are used only by Thimphu residents. Respondents in Thimphu reported using the Internet to make payments, transfer funds, print statements, and check account balances and foreign exchange rates. But Internet service is expensive in the capital, with a private connection costing Nu 399–2,999 (US$7.00–54.00) a month. Few people can afford personal connections, limiting opportunities for secure use of Internet banking services. Outside Thimphu, Internet penetration and use are very low.[4] Government offices offer service in some communities—as do a few Internet cafes, charging about Nu 50 (US$0.90) for an hour's use. Respondents considered the cost too high for the banking services they might receive over the Internet. Those who had tried to use the services found them to be too complicated, so they stopped.

Beyond ATM, mobile phone, and Internet banking technologies, other innovative strategies to expand financial access may also be worth considering. Branchless banking through agents, using both bank-based and non-bank-based models, is one solution for improving financial access in remote areas (see appendix H). The survey's findings suggest that branchless banking should not be limited to a non-bank-based model in which a mobile network operator offers services using agents as a distribution channel, but should also include bank-based models.

Notes

1. Each year households pay Nu 150 (US$3.00) for home insurance and Nu 45 (US$0.80) per person for life insurance. The maximum claim is Nu 100,000 (US$1,800) for damage to a home and Nu 15,000 (US$270) for a death. The office of the *gup* (the head of the municipality, or *gewog*) collects the premiums annually along with land, livestock, and other local taxes. The premiums are deposited with RICBL or with BIL (for home insurance).

2. Data are from the International Monetary Fund's 2011 Financial Access Survey. Given Bhutan's low population density and low coverage of bank branches (concentrated in urban areas), penetration averages should be interpreted with caution.

3. According to data from the Bhutan InfoComm and Media Authority and the National Statistics Bureau (NSB 2011), mobile phone subscribers represented almost 55 percent of the total population in 2010.

4. The International Telecommunication Union puts the number of Internet users in 2010 at around 7 percent of the population (as reported by Internet World Stats, "Bhutan Internet Usage, Broadband and Telecommunications Reports," http://www.internetworldstats.com/asia/bt.htm).

References

Financial Access Survey. 2011. International Monetary Fund, Washington, DC. http://fas.imf.org/.

NSB (National Statistics Bureau). 2011. *Statistical Yearbook of Bhutan 2011*. Thimphu: NSB.

World Bank. 2011. *Migration and Remittances Factbook*. 2nd ed. Washington, DC: World Bank.

Focus Group Survey Findings and Good Practices Informing Bhutan's Draft Financial Inclusion Policy

Objectives and recommendations in the draft policy[a]	Corresponding strategies and action points in the draft policy[a]	Good practices and survey findings[b]
Ensure that inclusive financial service providers play important roles toward the goal of financial inclusion[c]	• Set priority sector lending targets to mandate financial institutions to serve the target group (those with low access to financial services) • Develop joint strategy on how to promote financial inclusion, including by defining commitments with goals related to savings, insurance, payments, remittances, and loans and by drawing up a plan	*What does good practice suggest about serving priority sectors?* There are alternatives to priority sector lending that entail less risk. Indeed, directed credit can potentially have distorting effects on the entire economy. Setting a target for loans, for example, to rural areas or to the agricultural sector, without taking into account financial viability could weaken financial institutions and potentially crowd out credit to more productive sectors. Most experiences with directed lending in developing economies have been unsuccessful. The banks involved were often burdened by nonperforming loans, creating contingent liabilities for the budget. The risks (including low repayment rates, a weakening of financial discipline, and increased costs for funds for nonpriority sectors) suggest that less costly alternative policies should be prioritized. These alternative policies should create the market conditions needed to serve the priority sectors without public interventions.

Create an enabling regulatory environment for inclusive financial service providers	• In creating the enabling regulatory environment, ensure that it encompasses the operations of
	  ○ Non–deposit-taking microfinance institutions
	  ○ Deposit-taking microfinance institutions
	  ○ Nonbanks such as mobile network operators
	  ○ Branchless banking, to lower delivery costs
		What is the potential role of proportionate regulation?
		As highlighted by Demirgüç-Kunt, Beck, and Honohan (2008), regulators and supervisors play a key role in the design and implementation of an enabling environment for financial inclusion. Proportionate regulation (see CGAP 2010) can promote innovations that overcome barriers in expanding financial services at the same time that it maintains the safety and integrity of the financial system and ensures the protection of consumers. One example of proportionate regulation is Kenya's allowing the development of M-Pesa, the widely known mobile money transfer service reaching more than 15 million users in the country. Another is Brazil's relaxation of restrictions on agents—as access points for financial services—allowing every municipality in the country to have at least minimum access to financial services (World Bank 2012).

table continues next page

Objectives and recommendations in the draft policy[a]	Corresponding strategies and action points in the draft policy[a]	Good practices and survey findings[b]
Strengthen the capacity of inclusive financial service providers	• Facilitate access to funding for inclusive financial service providers • Strengthen the integrity of inclusive financial service providers (using ratings, audits, and the like) • Facilitate the capacity building of microfinance institutions in human resource development and technical service areas • Invite support from development partners (such as donor agencies)	*What are suggested priorities for supporting microfinance services?* Creating a critical mass of sustainable microfinance institutions, providing funds for microfinance institutions, ensuring their supervision, and supporting innovating infrastructure are essential. But an apex institution may not be the first-best solution for achieving these goals, since retail capacity is nonexistent in Bhutan and the potential size of the market is unknown. Sequencing seems better suited to the situation, starting with setting up a microfinance association to provide technical assistance to microfinance institutions, help them expand their business, and assist in their coordination.

Improve the availability of information on clients and potential clients	• Require the Credit Information Bureau to collect information on microfinance clients so as to help them
	  ◦ Reduce overindebtedness
	  ◦ Build a track record
	  ◦ Increase creditworthiness
	• Conduct market research on client demand
		What barriers do people face in access to formal financing?
		Among the main barriers that survey respondents identified are banks' requirements for high levels of collateral, in particular for immovable assets. Although a central registry is being established for secured transactions, there is no registry for movable assets, which would provide additional safeguards for lenders and expand opportunities for borrowing based on movable collateral.

Ensure the provision of quality and diverse financial products and services	• Support the development of quality financial products that are convenient, accessible, flexible, affordable, and responsive to clients' needs	*What types of financial services are people looking for that the formal sector is not providing?* Fieldwork identified a demand for financial services in several areas: • *Small, periodic savings and loan services.* Savers and borrowers expressed a need to deposit or borrow small amounts of cash periodically throughout the year. In particular, seasonal loans with repayments tied to the harvest or the sale of products would better reflect household cash flow and improve the likelihood of on-time repayments.

table continues next page

Objectives and recommendations in the draft policy[a]	Corresponding strategies and action points in the draft policy[a]	Good practices and survey findings[b]
		• *More accessible deposit and withdrawal services.* Depositing cash in banks is inconvenient for rural households, since there are no ATMs nearby allowing them to withdraw the cash when needed. Deposit mechanisms in the local community that accept small amounts and keep the cash accessible for later use would encourage account uptake.
		• *Flexible loan requirements.* Respondents expressed interest in noncollateralized loans, flexible term lengths, and deferred repayment periods. There was also much interest in expanding opportunities to receive education loans beyond households with a salaried employee.
		What are some insights into why informal financial services are filling the gaps left by the formal financial sector?
		Savings clubs and cooperatives. Group savings schemes and cooperatives are slowly emerging in Bhutan in response to the demand for saving locally and in small amounts. Savings clubs are run by community members who understand the savings capacity of contributors. Contributing savings to the groups is perceived as faster and more convenient than making deposits in banks.
		Insurance products. Lack of knowledge appears to be a big impediment to people's use of insurance services. While Bhutanese households are required to purchase life and home insurance, they rarely purchase other insurance products, and few people are aware of the types of insurance available. If more people understood insurance products, there would likely be greater demand for a tool that protects well-being during times of hardship.
		Remittances. Bhutanese households use remittances primarily to send money to family members within Bhutan and to students living in India. Among formal remittance channels, commercial banks and Bhutan Post are the most frequently used. But most rural areas lack access to formal channels and must rely instead on informal—and often expensive—service providers.

table continues next page

48

Objectives and recommendations in the draft policy[a]	Corresponding strategies and action points in the draft policy[a]	Good practices and survey findings[b]
		What does focusing on different segments of the population reveal about issues in access to financial services?
		Youth. Young people are underserved by formal financial services. Because most do not work and rely on their families for support, they fall out of the target client group for financial institutions. They also tend to self-exclude because of lack of experience and therefore self-confidence. Young people expressed a desire for access to youth education loans.
		Women. Women are integrated into family businesses and appear more willing than men to try new technology. And women tend to be knowledgeable about the financial products available, though the share of rural women using formal financial services is smaller than the share of rural entrepreneurs or farmers—men and women—doing so. A more precise understanding of women's needs, and financial products tailored to those needs, could increase women's financial inclusion. Field research suggests that women would favor smaller loan and deposit sizes, with repayment schedules tailored to their income cycles.
Empower clients to make informed choices	• Develop a financial literacy master plan (including financial education in school, university, and preservice curricula) • Require inclusive financial service providers to conduct financial education and set up counseling centers • Promote financial literacy and capability among the target group • Inculcate a savings culture into the target group	*What are priority areas for financial literacy education?* The savings strategies and attitudes among respondents suggest that Bhutanese households could benefit from financial literacy education, particularly in budgeting and cash flow. Although respondents identified long-term savings goals, households' strategies for reaching those goals are not consistent or well established. In addition, bank customers reported limited access to procedures, processes, and documents necessary for obtaining financial products.

table continues next page

Objectives and recommendations in the draft policy[a]	Corresponding strategies and action points in the draft policy[a]	Good practices and survey findings[b]
Make use of alternative delivery channels	• Require inclusive financial service providers to adopt branchless banking using agents, mobile phones, or card-reading devices • Attract new inclusive financial service providers	*What are people's perceptions of ATMs and mobile phone and Internet banking?* Respondents who use ATMs, mobile phone banking, and Internet banking services expressed interest in greater reliability of those services. For example, they expressed a need for installing more ATMs, maintaining those already in place (by ensuring that they are properly stocked with cash), and making sure that ATMs function properly (especially on weekends, when banks are closed). Mobile phones are widespread throughout the country, but mobile phone banking services are limited to text messages in English, and the use of these services is constrained by poor English-language literacy. Internet penetration is much lower, reducing people's interest in Internet-based banking services.

Protect clients	• Develop a comprehensive consumer protection regime
	
	• Pursue the concept of responsible finance through such means as
	  ○ A code of conduct
	  ○ Social impact measurement
	
	• Improve the target group's understanding of consumer protection measures
		How aware are households of consumer protection mechanisms?
		Most consumers are unaware of consumer protection mechanisms now in place. Those aware of the option of pursuing a lawsuit see it as a costly and time-consuming one that is not worth the effort. Households would welcome consumer protection mechanisms that allow them to obtain redress in a nonconfrontational manner. In addition, survey respondents highlighted a need for financial institutions to make information available in local languages.

table continues next page

Objectives and recommendations in the draft policy[a]	Corresponding strategies and action points in the draft policy[a]	Good practices and survey findings[b]
Expand microfinance opportunities to reach the underserved	• Microfinance institutions are among the inclusive financial service providers expected to reach the underserved, as described above.	*Do the borrowing practices of households indicate a need for formal microfinance services?* Many Bhutanese rely on informal lenders—most often, family, friends, or moneylenders—for quick, small loans for investment capital or for emergencies and immediate needs. Most households that borrow from informal providers do not attempt to borrow from financial institutions, mainly because bank products do not meet their needs. Even households with some access to the formal financial sector continue to use informal financing mechanisms. Because informal lending is illegal in Bhutan, however, the processes and procedures for accessing an informal loan go unregulated. The findings of the field research highlight a need for formal microfinance services providing small group and individual loans with flexible repayments.
Establish a mechanism for regular reviews and updates of the Financial Inclusion Policy	• Set up data collection and monitoring mechanism	*What is good practice in monitoring financial inclusion?* Worldwide, practitioners measure financial inclusion through indicators collecting information from users (demand side) as well as from providers (supply side) (World Bank 2012). Consistent with recommended good practice, Bhutan's national Living Standard Survey now includes financial inclusion questions (see appendix C) and will help collect nationally representative financial inclusion data every five years. International data collection efforts can help in comparing financial inclusion in Bhutan with relevant benchmarks. One such initiative is the Global Financial Inclusion (Global Findex) Database, a new public database available since April 2012 that can be used to track progress in improving access to financial services.

a. Refers to a preliminary, August 2012 draft of the Financial Inclusion Policy.

b. The survey findings reflected here include results from both focus group discussions and in-depth interviews carried out in the Bhutan Financial Inclusion Focus Group Survey.

c. The draft Financial Inclusion Policy defines inclusive financial service providers as banks, nonbank financial institutions, microfinance institutions, cooperatives, NGOs, and nonbanks such as mobile network operators.

References

CGAP (Consultative Group to Assist the Poor). 2010. "Global Standard-Setting Bodies and Financial Inclusion for the Poor: Toward Proportionate Standards and Guidance." http://www.cgap.org/publications/global-standard-setting-bodies-and-financial-inclusion-poor.

Demirgüç-Kunt, A., T. Beck, and P. Honohan. 2008. *Finance for All? Policies and Pitfalls in Expanding Access.* Washington, DC: World Bank. http://siteresources.worldbank.org/INTFINFORALL/Resources/4099583-1194373512632/FFA_book.pdf.

Global Financial Inclusion (Global Findex) Database. World Bank, Washington, DC. http://www.worldbank.org/globalfindex.

World Bank. 2012. *Financial Inclusion Strategies—Reference Framework.* Washington, DC: World Bank. http://siteresources.worldbank.org/EXTFINANCIALSECTOR/Resources/282884-1339624653091/8703882-1339624678024/8703850-133962469 5396/FI-Strategies-ReferenceFramework-FINAL.pdf.

Selected Examples of Financial Inclusion Strategies

Country	Baseline data	Targets	Strategy: agreement on financial inclusion goal	Policy and regulatory reforms: removal of regulatory barriers	Financial sector response: new services and delivery mechanisms	Government monitoring body
Brazil	• Financial Inclusion Report	• Expand basic financial services to all municipalities	• National Partnership for Financial Inclusion	• New regulations broadening range of services that can be offered by correspondent banks	• Correspondent banking model • Simplified current and savings accounts • Mobile phone financial services • Call centers for consumer protection	• Progress monitored by Financial Inclusion Unit (Banco Central do Brasil)
India	• All-India Debt and Investment Survey (undertaken every 10 years) • National Sample Survey • Reserve Bank of India and other survey data from research institutes	• Provide financial services (including credit) through regional rural banks and rural or semiurban branches of commercial banks to at least 50 percent of financially excluded households in the country by 2012 and to the rest by 2015	• 12th Five-Year Plan • Statements of intent signed between Ministry of Finance and public sector banks • Financial inclusion plans submitted to Reserve Bank of India • National Rural Financial Inclusion Plan • Financial Inclusion Committee constituted by government	• Regulatory freedom to open rural and semiurban bank branches • Guidelines issued for banking correspondent and banking facilitator model for microfinance • Simplification of procedures for access to finance (such as "know your customer" guidelines, and no due certificates from other banks) • Microfinance circular • Numerous circulars relating to rural and cooperative banking and to priority-sector lending for all commercial banks	• Basic bank accounts, no-frill bank accounts • Banking agents • Use of country's extensive post office network to further the financial inclusion agenda • Experimentation with delivery models, financing mechanisms, products, and technologies (such as low-cost ATMs, biometric cards, and mobile phones) • Banks launching mobile van banking facilities in small villages • Partnership model allowing banks to leverage microfinance institutions' loan origination capability	• Reserve Bank of India's guidance on financial inclusion, Khan Commission

table continues next page

Country	Baseline data	Targets	Strategy: agreement on financial inclusion goal	Policy and regulatory reforms: removal of regulatory barriers	Financial sector response: new services and delivery mechanisms	Government monitoring body
Indonesia	• Access to Finance Household Survey of Migrant Workers	• Diversify and expand financial services offered to households	• National Strategy for Financial Inclusion	• Development of Bank of Indonesia's *sharia* banking policies • Credit Guarantee Policy Regulations	• Expansion of ATM network • State-owned pawn company to give loans against movable assets • Indonesian post office operating in mobile service vehicles and with village agents	• Responsibility of Office of the Vice President
Kenya	• National Financial Access Survey (FinAccess)	• Increase savings and investment from 14 percent of GDP to 25–30 percent • Deepen penetration of financial services, especially to rural areas • Double formal financial inclusion to 50 percent of population	• Comprehensive Financial Sector Reform and Development Strategy • Financial Access Partnership	• Microfinance Act and Regulations • Banking Act • Credit information sharing • Proceeds of Crime and Anti-Money-Laundering Act • Regulatory framework for savings and credit cooperatives • Public sector signaling space for innovation (not rushing to regulate mobile banking before model is tested) • Regulators encouraging competition through compilation and dissemination of regulatory framework	• Mobile banking (M-Pesa); new mobile-phone-based money transfer products • Post offices and banking agents • Credit information sharing • Government payments program • Emergence of specialized providers (such as PayNet, a national system of ATMs) to a wide range of banks and other financial institutions	• Central Bank of Kenya

table continues next page

Country	Baseline data	Targets	Strategy: agreement on financial inclusion goal	Policy and regulatory reforms: removal of regulatory barriers	Financial sector response: new services and delivery mechanisms	Government monitoring body
Peru	• Financial surveys to measure financial literacy, access, and use of financial services • Set of financial inclusion indicators on access, use, and geographic inequality distribution	• Raise level of knowledge about financial services, especially among low-income households	• Planned	• Financial System Act and Insurance • Consumer protection regulation	• Banking agents • Financial literacy programs (Programa de Asesoría a Docentes, Virtual Classroom website)	• Committee on Financial Inclusion, with monitoring based on financial inclusion indicators collected • Financial Touch-Point Access—planned indicator to provide information on relationship between financial inclusion and economic well-being

Source: World Bank 2012.

Reference

World Bank. 2012. *Financial Inclusion Strategies—Reference Framework*. Washington, DC: World Bank. http://siteresources.worldbank.org/EXTFINANCIALSECTOR/ Resources/282884-1339624653091/8703882-1339624678024/8703850-13396246 95396/FI-Strategies-ReferenceFramework-FINAL.pdf.

Financial Inclusion Questionnaire in Bhutan Living Standard Survey 2012

Question	Answers
1 Do you or does anyone in your household currently have a savings or deposit account?	No Yes. Name household member (husband, wife, etc.). Type of account: a. Savings b. Current banking c. Debit/credit/ATM card d. Other (specify) _____
2 Has anyone in your household applied for a loan from a financial institution, NGO, or moneylender in the last two years?	No Yes. Name household member. From: a. Bank b. BDBL c. RICBL/BIL d. Supplier/shop e. Relatives/friends f. Moneylender g. Nongovernmental organization h. Other (specify) _____ (pawnshop, etc.)
3 How do you send or receive money?	a. Not applicable b. Family and friends c. Money transfer service d. Post office money order e. Directly into bank account f. Check g. Other (specify) _____
4 What is the main household option for emergencies?	a. Use own savings b. Borrow from family c. Borrow from supplier d. Borrow from moneylender e. Borrow from savings committee f. Liquidate assets (sell livestock) g. Pawnshop h. Other (specify) _____

table continues next page

Question	Answers
5 What insurance products do you use?	a. None b. Life insurance c. Health insurance d. Crop insurance e. Property insurance (assets, livestock, housing) f. Other (specify)____
6 What is the predominant way household members keep savings or extra cash?	a. Not applicable b. Safe place in house c. With relatives or friends d. Savings committee or cooperative e. Convert to asset (jewelry, livestock, land) f. At the bank Other (specify) ____

Source: National Statistics Bureau.

Technical Note on Focus Group Survey in Bhutan

The purpose of the Bhutan Financial Inclusion Focus Group Survey was to understand the reality of access to finance at the household level, particularly in rural areas; to identify potential demand-side constraints in expanding access to finance, such as lack of knowledge and awareness among the Bhutanese population of financial products and services and financial service providers; and to provide results that would feed into the policy and planning work of the Financial Inclusion Policy process. The survey was carried out in spring 2012 through focus group discussions and follow-up interviews in four Bhutanese communities. The focus group discussions were aimed at exploring five main issues:

- Actual use of financial products and services
- Potential needs for financial products and services
- Physical access to financial products and services
- Financial literacy and capability
- Consumer protection

Site Selection

Site selection was based on a methodology used for a Rapid Qualitative Assessment completed in Bhutan in January 2011. In selecting data collection sites, two main criteria were taken into consideration: socioeconomic character-istics (whether rural or urban and whether more economically vibrant or less economically vibrant) and geographic distribution. The main references used were a poverty map (NSB and World Bank 2010) and stratified data on urban and rural populations from the 2005 Population and Housing Census of Bhutan (NSB 2006). In addition, the Planning Commission Secretariat of Bhutan had identified 27 urban areas in the country (all 20 district headquarters; 2 subdistricts, Gelephu and Phuntsholing; and 5 satellite towns, Bondey, Gedu, Khaling, Ranjung, and Warmong). For practical purposes, all places other than those categorized as urban were defined as rural. Site selection was reviewed with the Royal Monetary Authority and the Financial Inclusion Policy Working Group.

On the basis of socioeconomic characteristics and geographic distribution, four districts in Bhutan were selected for data collection:

- Thimphu—urban, more economically vibrant, in the west
- Mongar—urban, less economically vibrant, in the east
- Paro—rural, more economically vibrant, in the west
- Samtse—rural, less economically vibrant, in the south

Within each district a specific community was then selected for the study.

The city of Thimphu was selected as the *urban, more economically vibrant site* for data collection on the basis of several indicators. Located in the western part of the country, it is the capital city and is also among the most urbanized parts of Bhutan. According to the 2005 census, Thimphu district has the largest urban population: 79,185, accounting for 80.3 percent of the district's total population. According to the national newspaper *Kuensel* (September 1, 2009), about a fifth of Bhutan's total population lives in Thimphu district, which brings together people from all regions and cultural backgrounds in the country.[1]

As home to most government ministries and head offices for government departments and corporations, Thimphu district has one of the most literate populations in the country. Indeed, it has the highest youth and adult literacy rate, at 69 percent (NSB 2008). Statistics show that Thimphu also leads in economic opportunities, employment, education, health, and infrastructure. Compared with other districts, Thimphu has the largest number of industrial firms (6,035 micro, small, medium-size, and large firms) and the largest number of employed people (36,116) (NSB 2009). Most areas of Thimphu (about 90 percent) have a poverty rate in the 0–15 percent range (NSB and World Bank 2010). But with urbanization also come social ills, and Thimphu has the highest reported crime rate as well as the highest youth unemployment rate in the country.

By contrast, Paro, located in the western region, is one of the least urbanized districts, with an urban population of 2,932 (8.2 percent of the district's total population) according to the 2005 census. Paro is also economically vibrant, and within this district the community of Shaba was chosen as the *rural, more economically vibrant site*. Paro has a strong agricultural base, with the largest cultivated area in the country for principal agricultural products such as wheat and the second largest for paddy and barley (NSB 2009). Its farms are more mechanized than those in other districts, and its people have higher living standards. Social institutions such as schools, banking, health facilities, communication facilities, and agricultural extension facilities are well developed.

Moreover, while identified as rural on the basis of the size of its urban population, Paro has the third largest number of industrial firms (1,270) after

Thimphu and Chukha districts (NSB 2009). All areas of Paro district have a poverty rate in the 0–15 percent range (NSB and World Bank 2010).

The town of Mongar was selected as the *urban, less economically vibrant site.* Located in the east, Mongar was chosen so as to provide wider coverage of the country. Mongar is among the largest towns in the east and is fairly developed, though far less developed than such places as Thimphu, Paro, and Phuntsholing. Mongar is centrally located and is the hub for eastern regions. Its culture, traditions, and agricultural practices differ from those of the west and south. Communities speak Sharchop, a dialect widely spoken in the east.

The 2005 census identifies the district of Mongar as the second most urbanized in eastern Bhutan, after Samdrupjongkhar. But Mongar is considered less economically vibrant: it has 664 industrial firms, compared with 917 in Samdrupjongkhar (NSB 2009). Most areas in Mongar have a poverty rate in the 52–69 percent or 37–51 percent range (NSB and World Bank 2010).

Within the district of Samtse, the community of Chengmari was selected as the *rural, less economically vibrant site.* Samtse is located in the south and, like Mongar, was chosen so as to have wider coverage of the country. Samtse was preferred over other southern districts because its communities are still less developed overall. Samtse is also less developed than the other survey sites. All areas in Samtse have a poverty rate in the 52–69 percent or 37–51 percent range (NSB and World Bank 2010). Large parts of the district remain unconnected to roads and other infrastructure.

Survey Tools

In each community selected, four focus group discussions were undertaken, each with at least 10 participants (table D.1). Focus group participants in each community were segmented into four groups:

- Young adults (18–24 years old)
- Women
- Employed and self-employed individuals and entrepreneurs in nonfarm activities
- Subsistence farmers and unemployed people

In addition to the focus group discussions, eight follow-up individual interviews (two in each focus group) were carried out in each district. These interviews were intended to provide in-depth analysis of a finding that emerged from the focus group discussions as important for understanding gender norms or roles shaping economic decisions in the locality. The focus group discussions and interviews were conducted in March–April 2012 (table D.2).

The questionnaires used to carry out the survey were based on the financial consumer protection diagnostic undertaken by the World Bank in Nicaragua in September 2011 and consumer research and global good practices from

Table D.1 Data Collection Tools and Respondents in Focus Group Survey in Bhutan

Data collection method	Time required	Purpose	Respondents in each community[a]
Activity 1: four focus group discussions in each of four communities (16 in total)	1.5 hours per focus group discussion	To explore • Actual use of financial products and services • Potential needs for financial products and services • Physical access to financial products and services • Financial literacy and capability • Consumer protection	• One focus group of 10 young adults • One focus group of 10 women • One focus group of 10 employed or self-employed individuals or entrepreneurs • One focus group of 10 farmers or unemployed individuals
Activity 2: eight individual interviews in each community (32 in total)	1 hour per interview	To provide in-depth analysis of a finding that emerges as important for understanding gender norms or roles shaping economic decisions in the locality	• Eight follow-up interviews (two per focus group)

a. While 10 was the minimum number of participants for each focus group, some focus groups included more (see table 1.1 in chapter 1). The three non-gender-based focus groups included both women and men.

Table D.2 Schedule for Focus Group Survey in Bhutan

Dates	Activity
March 12–13	Finalization of survey tools
March 14	Training for the survey team
March 19–26	Fieldwork in Chengmari (Samtse) and finalization of community report
March 26–April 12	Fieldwork in Mongar and finalization of community report
April 12–23	Fieldwork in Thimphu and finalization of community report
April 23–May 1	Fieldwork in Shaba (Paro) and finalization of community report
May 1–June 4	Preparation and finalization of national synthesis report

the World Bank's financial inclusion practice. Questionnaires were reviewed by the Royal Monetary Authority and the Financial Inclusion Policy Working Group.

Framework for Taking Stock of Financial Inclusion

The analysis of results from the focus group discussions and interviews is informed by the World Bank's reference framework for financial inclusion strategies (World Bank 2012). The reference framework builds on country models and examples as well as the work of the Global Partnership for Financial Inclusion, the Alliance for Financial Inclusion, the International Finance Corporation of the World Bank Group, Consultative Group to Assist the Poor (CGAP), the World Bank, the United Nations Capital Development Fund, Asia-Pacific Economic Cooperation, and others. The framework identifies the diagnostic phase as the first step in developing a comprehensive financial inclusion strategy. A stocktaking diagnostic that highlights the financial needs and capabilities of consumers can strengthen policy development by tailoring the development of new financial services to the preferences of the financially excluded (figure D.1).

The reference framework identifies three aspects of a comprehensive assessment of financial inclusion:

- Access to financial products and services—which products are available to consumers
- Use of financial products and services—how much or how often consumers use the products
- Quality of financial products and services—consumers' ability to benefit from the financial products on the market

Information about these three aspects together can help ensure that a strategy for increasing financial inclusion moves beyond creating new financial products and services and instead ensures that the products and services created respond to financial consumers' needs. This framework is used as the basis of analysis in the demand-side assessment of financial inclusion in Bhutan.

Figure D.1 Responsible Financial Inclusion Strategies

Consumer protection and financial literacy help build public confidence and raise demand for financial services Disclosure and transparency promote financial inclusion, lower risk, and can stimulate competition Financial literacy enables consumers to benefit from financial decisions	
Financial inclusion	**Financial inclusion combined with financial capability, consumer protection**
Examples of how households and firms can benefit	Examples of how households and firms can benefit
Microinsurance: Microenterprises able to buy insurance that reduces exposure to potential losses and enables business growth	**Microinsurance:** Microenterprises able to understand the risks covered, to compare the cost of premium with potential benefit, and to select the most appropriate product
Basic bank accounts: Low-income households able to open a "no frills" bank account, accessed through a mobile phone or ATMs, to save, receive remittances, make payments	**Basic bank accounts:** Low-income households able to select a bank account that meets their needs and enables them to lower financial transaction costs and to avoid hidden charges or excessive debt with credit cards
Regulatory reforms: Regulators introduce reforms to promote innovation by financial institutions to serve lower-income clients	**Regulatory reforms:** Regulators better understand and accommodate the level of understanding of consumers, ensuring that reforms have the maximum impact on the intended consumers

Source: World Bank 2012, 14.

Note

1. The Ministry of Labour and Human Resources of the Royal Government of Bhutan (2011) estimates the country's total population at 713,300.

References

Ministry of Labour and Human Resources of the Royal Government of Bhutan. 2011. *Labour Force Survey Report 2011*. Department of Employment, Thimphu.

NSB (National Statistics Bureau). 2006. *Results of Population & Housing Census of Bhutan 2005*. Thimphu: NSB.

———. 2008. *Socio-Economic and Demographic Indicators 2005*. Thimphu: NSB.

———. 2009. *Statistical Yearbook of Bhutan 2009*. Thimphu: NSB.

NSB (National Statistics Bureau) and World Bank. 2010. "Small Area Estimation of Poverty in Rural Bhutan." Technical Report, NSB, Thimphu; and Economic Policy and Poverty Unit, South Asia Region, World Bank, Washington, DC.

World Bank. 2012. *Financial Inclusion Strategies—Reference Framework*. Washington, DC: World Bank. http://siteresources.worldbank.org/EXTFINANCIALSECTOR/ Resources/282884-1339624653091/8703882-1339624678024/8703850-13396246 95396/FI-Strategies-ReferenceFramework-FINAL.pdf.

Field Guide for Focus Group Survey in Bhutan

This field guide was designed to serve as an easy-to-use manual for conducting the focus group discussions and individual interviews in the Bhutan Financial Inclusion Focus Group Survey.

Focus Group Discussion Guide

Please complete the following profile for the participants in the focus group discussion.

Participants' Profile

	Name	Gender	Age	Level of education	Occupation
1					
2					
3					
4					
5					
6					
7					
8					
9					
10					

Please cover the following topics in the focus group discussion.

1. **Awareness of formal and informal financial service providers and their products and services**
   - Who are the players—formal and informal (financial institutions, associations, cooperatives, religious institutions, individuals, etc.)?

- What are the formal and informal products and services available—deposits (saving, current, fixed, recurring, etc.), loans (individual and group), remittances (payments, receipts), credit and debit cards, overdraft facilities, letters of credit, insurance, and others?
- How do the respondents know about the players, products, and services—through use, family, friends, media, etc.?

2. **Use of both formal and informal products and services**

- Who uses it? Why? Their experiences, their opinion of the products, terms and conditions, and other details. Details on requirements, time, and cost to obtain the services. Trends on use—and why? Do banks offer loan products that reflect the needs of the community?
- Access—use in relation to physical distance and affordability. Number of households that have access. Who currently has access to a financial service but is not using it.
- Physical access—details on distance from the financial institutions.
- Other access issues: Affordability (*considered one of the greatest barriers to access*). Quality of financial services (*describes products for which the price is in line with the client's ability to pay for them*).

a. *Formal products and services*

- Saving—amount, purpose, how, where (choice of institutions, experiences—personal and from other acquaintances respondents are aware of, savings potential of the segment, different schemes). Deposits—saving, current, fixed, recurring, etc.
- Borrowing—both from banks and from microfinance institutions (choice of institutions, requirements, experiences—personal and others, satisfaction with the product and service provided, cost and time taken to obtain the service, feedback). Do banks offer loan products that reflect the needs of the community? If not, what is the potential gap or need? Purpose of the borrowing, any difficulties faced—charges, distances, intimidation, time waiting in line, etc. Have respondents been asked for guarantors or collateral? (Discuss to investigate details of the guarantors, guarantees, or both.)
- Remittances (choice of institutions, experiences—personal and others). Do participants use or need remittance services and what type of remittances (formal; domestic, regional, or international; amounts received or remitted per year). How much on average is the amount of money respondents received? Remittances—sending, receiving, payment, etc. Amount and frequencies—satisfaction with the services or any bad or good experiences, etc. Postal services, Western Union, MoneyGram, etc.
- Insurance (choice of institutions, experiences—personal or others). What products are insured? What are insurance needs? What are the premiums, who are the players, and what products do they offer?
- Internet, mobile, ATM card, text message reminders, and others.

- Do cooperative associations exist that facilitate financing for crops, sale of harvest, etc.? Ask about NGOs such as Tarayana.

b. *Informal products and services*

- Saving—amount, purpose, how, where, why (choice of institutions, experiences—personal or others). Some people do not save at all; those who save might do it in different ways. Do respondents regularly have money left over after they have paid for food and other necessary items? What do they do with any money they have left? What are the main obstacles for them to open an informal or formal savings account (minimum balances, charges, distances, or being afraid of entering a bank branch)? Saving—keeping money under the mattress; investing in gold or livestock, etc.; saving through groups or cooperatives, etc.
- Borrowing from informal moneylenders—associations, cooperatives, monastic bodies, family and friends, etc. (choice of institutions, experiences—personal or others). What are requirements, terms and conditions, who are lenders and borrowers, why go into informal borrowing, good or bad stories.
- Time and cost to obtain such facilities. What are respondents' opinions about these products? What is the purpose of borrowing? In case of default, what happens—what are the repayment mode, amounts, and other requirements?
- Remittances (choice of institutions, experiences—personal or others), potential need, who uses it, amount, frequencies, etc.
- Do cooperative associations exist that facilitate financing for crops, sale of harvest, etc.?

3. Choice of formal and informal services

- Discuss opinions on the products and services, any other feedback.

4. Access to mobile phones and the Internet

- Use of facilities in that area. Does the respondent own or use a mobile phone? Does the respondent use it to make bank transactions? If yes, for which banking services (checking balance, making payment, purchasing goods, remittances, other)? Why is the respondent not using a mobile phone to make transactions (cost, security, difficulty, reliability, never heard about this, etc.)? Is there Internet access in the community? If not, where is the closest access?
- Level of mobile and Internet penetration and use? Would the respondents feel comfortable using their mobile phones to undertake transactions? Are any payments (or bartering) already taking place with mobile phones?

5. Client protection

- The debt collection practices of providers should be neither abusive nor coercive. Do providers treat clients with dignity and not deprive them of the ability to earn their livelihood?

- Transparency (complete disclosure of information by a financial service provider—includes full disclosure of all pricing, terms, and conditions of products in a form understandable to clients).
- Fair and respectful treatment of clients; privacy of client data; and mechanisms for complaint resolution.
- Redress of grievances—a client protection principle. Do service providers have in place timely and responsive mechanisms for resolving complaints and problems of individual clients?
- Employees of financial service providers should comply with high ethical standards in their interactions with clients, and providers should ensure that adequate safeguards are in place to detect and correct corruption or mistreatment of clients.

6. Financial literacy and capability

- Check the knowledge, understanding, skills, attitudes, and especially behaviors that people need in order to make sound personal finance decisions, suited to their social and financial circumstances. Check the ability to understand how to use financial products and services and how to manage personal, household, or microenterprise finances over time.

7. Potential need

- Every community report should try to come up with at least one paragraph on potential need. If there is no potential need, why not? Potential need means market. Appropriate financial services—what is being offered by financial institutions, and what is the need of the participants? Look at the types of financial products offered, their terms and conditions—collateral, loan period, flexibility, etc. Does what is offered suit what people need?

Individual Interview Guide

Please try to cover topics on access to finance that were not covered in the focus group discussion or topics that were mentioned or discussed in the focus group discussion but for which further detail is needed. Sensitive questions can be asked in the individual interviews. Try not to duplicate information that is in the focus group discussion. Possible topics include these:

- Trends
- Head of the family
- Potential need
- Whether access to banks has become easier or more difficult in the last 10 years or is unchanged. What feature did change?

Two Successful Community-Driven Savings Initiatives

Community-based savings organizations have served as a cost-effective mechanism of financial inclusion for rural households throughout the world. Many are rotating savings and credit associations (ROSCAs) or accumulating savings and credit associations (ASCAs). These are often indigenously formed organizations that assist households in achieving savings goals by requiring members to make regular contributions to a communal pot. The contributions are then distributed to members in a rotating fashion, with each member in turn receiving the total contributions (ROSCAs) or a share of them (ASCAs).

Mata Masu Dubara Program in Rural Niger

One ASCA initiative that has been very successful, and widely replicated, is the Mata Masu Dubara program in rural Niger, funded by the NGO CARE (Grant and Henry 2007). The program centers on women—Mata Masu Dubara means "women on the move" in Hausa. It has led to the creation of more than 5,500 active, stand-alone women's groups, serving more than 162,000 women in rural Niger. The groups provide financial services to their members, managing total savings of US$3 million.

The Mata Masu Dubara methodology is aimed at promoting time-bound ASCAs. These accumulate savings and set up credit associations during a well-defined period, which can run from 9 to 12 months. At the end of the cycle a group can decide to distribute the savings among its members or use the funds for a group activity. Indeed, a group activity, such as the creation of a grain bank, can be the main motivation for an ASCA. The end of the cycle also represents an opportunity to renew group memberships: current members can exercise their right to leave, while new members can join. Impact assessments note that the overwhelming majority of groups (about

95 percent) continue their operations, often increasing the amount of their weekly contributions.

The groups have received training from support organizations, based on a four-phase curriculum, on how to better operate their ASCA.[1] In Niger 500 trainers selected by their communities receive training themselves, then monitor the groups and develop new ones. The group members pay for these services, and sustainability is achieved through fees paid by the groups rather than interest charged by a microfinance institution.[2]

Based on a simple and appropriately adapted savings-based product, the model makes it easy to achieve sustainability and replication of the associations. The Mata Masu Dubara program is sustainable because each group is autonomous. Strong ownership, good governance, and transparency are also critical to the success of the program. It builds on local capacities and is adapted to a wide range of local cultural settings.

The Mata Masu Dubara model has been replicated in many other countries, such as Mali and Zambia, and it is being implemented in Latin America by such agencies as the U.S. Peace Corps. The methodology, which evolved slowly over time, has served as the starting point for all other village savings and loan programs.

Village Savings and Loan Associations in Zanzibar

Zanzibar's village savings and loan associations are another successful initiative (Johnson and others 2007). These have been showcased as a savings group model that has shown remarkable adaptability and resilience in challenging settings (CARE 2011). Modeled on the Mata Masu Dubara program in Niger, the village savings and loan associations in Zanzibar are time-bound ASCAs. Each group consists of 15–30 people who save regularly and borrow from the group fund. Loans are repaid with interest and have a term of usually one to three months. The cycle can last about a year, after which the financial assets are divided among the members in proportion to each one's savings. The groups normally re-form immediately and start a new cycle of saving and lending.

As in the Mata Masu Dubara program in Niger, the groups are self-financed: they rely solely on their own savings and have no access to external funds (except for training similar to that in the Mata Masu Dubara model). An evaluation of Zanzibar's village savings and loan associations shows that they have provided useful and sustainable financial services to communities poorly served by other organizations (Johnson and others 2007). Membership in the associations has grown rapidly. But in considering how the approach might work in other settings, the relatively high socioeconomic status of the members—especially the relatively large share with secondary education—needs to be taken into account. The model's performance might be less easily replicable in poorer and less educated environments.

Notes

1. During the first three months a trainer visits the groups every week and trains them in group dynamics. This is followed by another three months of less frequent visits, generally every two weeks, as the groups become more independent. The visits are scaled back to once a month after 6 months and cease after 12–18 months.

2. For more details, see Allen (2002).

References

Allen, H. 2002. "CARE International's Village Savings & Loan Programmes in Africa: Micro Finance for the Rural Poor That Works." https://www.msu.edu/unit/phl/devconference/CAREVillSavLoanAfr.pdf.

CARE. 2011. *Microfinance in Africa: State-of-the-Sector Report—Closing the Gap.* http://www.care.org/getinvolved/advocacy/access-africa/pdf/CARE-Access-Africa-Closing-the-Gap-2011.pdf.

Grant, W. J., and C. A. Henry. 2007. "CARE's Mata Masu Dubara (Women on the Move) Program in Niger: Successful Financial Intermediation in the Rural Sahel." *Journal of Microfinance* 4 (2): 189–216.

Johnson, S., E. Anyango, E. Esipisu, M. Malkamaki, C. Musoke, and L. Opoku. 2007. "Village Savings and Loan Associations: Experience from Zanzibar." *Small Enterprise Development Journal* 18 (1): 11–24.

Summary of Terms and Conditions for Formal and Informal Lending in Bhutan

Formal lending (by banks and nonbank financial institutions)	Informal lending (by moneylenders)
Providers Formal financial service providers in the four survey locations include five banks: Bank of Bhutan Limited (BOB), Bhutan Development Bank Limited (BDBL), Bhutan National Bank Limited, Druk Punjab National Bank Limited, and T Bank. The others are Bhutan Insurance Limited, the National Pension and Provident Fund, and the Royal Insurance Corporation of Bhutan Limited.	In the rural survey locations informal lenders include wealthy landowners, former government officials, retired public servants or corporate employees, community leaders or officials, senior monks (*dragays*), lay monks, religious institutions, and monastic bodies. In the urban locations they include contractors, large business owners, civil servants, corporate employees, businessmen, and gamblers.
Loan amount Loan amounts depend on the type of loan. Participants reported formal loans ranging from Nu 7,500 (US$135) to Nu 20 million (US$360,000).	Informal loans are usually small, in amounts below Nu 50,000 (US$900). But they are sometimes larger, and one participant reported borrowing Nu 3 million (US$54,000).
Loan period Loan periods also depend on the type of loan, ranging from 1 year to 25 years (with the longest for housing loans).	Loan periods range from one month to one year, though depending on the loan amount and the agreement between the borrower and lender, a loan might also be taken for five to six years.
Interest rate According to participants, interest rates depend on the type of loan and range from 10 to 15 percent a year.	Informal lenders charge very high interest rates, ranging from 2 to 10 percent a month.

table continues next page

Formal lending (by banks and nonbank financial institutions)	Informal lending (by moneylenders)

Documentation requirements

Survey participants reported that obtaining a loan from a financial institution usually entails long and cumbersome procedures. The documents required depend on the loan type and amount. They generally include the loan application form, a letter from the village head (for a rural loan from BDBL), an original ownership certificate (for land, a house, or a vehicle), a business license, a photocopy of the borrower's citizen identity card, two passport-size photographs, legal stamps, the borrower's latest pay slip (for a government employee loan), and guarantor details in case additional collateral is required.

For a loan for purchasing agricultural machinery (such as a water pump or threshing machine), the application must be routed through the subdistrict (*geog*) and district (*dzongkhag*) administration.

For a housing construction loan, a borrower needs to submit a construction approval letter from the municipal corporation or district administration, engineering and architectural drawings, and a construction cost estimate.

According to participants, moneylenders usually lend to people whom they know and in most cases provide the loans after drawing up a simple agreement with the borrower. In some cases they may also require the borrower to submit a photocopy of identification or provide witnesses. Participants also reported that a moneylender will forgo the agreement if the amount borrowed is small (below Nu 30,000, or US$540) and the borrower is a reliable person with a good borrowing record with the lender.

Processing time and cost

The time for processing a formal loan depends on the amount and also varies from bank to bank. In general, loans are granted within a month if the borrower can submit all the documents required. The longest processing time reported was three months, for a housing loan.

A participant from Thimphu reported a processing time of one month for a loan of Nu 6.5 million (US$117,000). Expenses incurred amounted to roughly Nu 8,000 (US$144), for travel, accommodation, food, legal fees, technical fees, and Credit Information Bureau charges. Another reported a processing time of one month, and expenses of roughly Nu 10,000 (US$180), to get a loan of Nu 3 million (US$54,000). A farmer from Mongar reported incurring an estimated cost of Nu 5,000 (US$90) for a loan of Nu 500,000 (US$9,000).

Processing times for group loans are much shorter. A group loan from BDBL for Nu 50,000 (US$900) was processed within two days. The reported cost was about Nu 200 (US$3.60), for travel, photocopying, and legal stamps. For an orchard development loan of Nu 30,000 (US$540) from BDBL, the processing time was about one week and the cost about Nu 500 (US$9).

A respondent from Paro reported that for a vehicle loan of Nu 700,000 (US$12,600) from BOB, the processing time was 10 days and the cost about Nu 1,500 (US$27).

Because informal lenders usually know their clients personally, the process for obtaining an informal loan is simple and takes much less time. Participants said that in most cases informal loans are given on the spot or at most within a week. The easy access, fast service, and limited formalities are among the reasons that people choose informal loans.

The reported cost for processing an informal loan is minimal, from as little as Nu 40 (US$0.72) to a few hundred ngultrum—for legal stamps, a photocopy of the borrower's identity card, and small informal gifts.

table continues next page

Formal lending (by banks and nonbank financial institutions)	Informal lending (by moneylenders)
Collateral requirements	
Formal financial institutions require assets such as land, a house, a vehicle, or machinery as collateral for a loan. BDBL will accept land or a house outside the municipality, but other banks require collateral that is in a commercial area. Financial institutions do not accept wetlands or *tseri* (land used for shifting cultivation) as collateral. In addition to collateral, formal lenders sometimes also require a guarantor (someone with assets, a good borrowing record, and a regular job and steady income).	Informal lenders usually do not require collateral. But they may in some cases, especially if the loan is large (as in the case of a loan for gambling reported by a participant from Thimphu). In these cases the collateral might be expensive jewelry, a vehicle, a house, or land. In other cases an informal lender might require a guarantor rather than collateral.
For loans through BDBL's group guarantee lending schemes, popular in farming communities, borrowers do not need collateral because members stand as surety for one another.	Participants from Samtse reported that collateral requirements for informal loans are quite flexible. Lenders might require fixed assets such as land or require a guarantor—but would also accept other forms of collateral, such as cattle, jewelry, or part of the harvest. In some cases, if the loan is small or the lender knows the borrower, no collateral is required.
For government employee loans, lenders take provident funds (retirement benefits) as collateral in addition to requiring a guarantor.	
Repayments	
Payments of formal loans are made monthly, quarterly, semiannually, or annually.	Payments on informal loans are flexible. Typically, interest is paid monthly, and principal is paid at the end of the term agreed on. But this may vary. Participants reported cases in which all payments were made at the end of the loan period.
	In some communities, such as in Samtse, informal loans may be repaid in kind. Participants said that people borrowing from wealthy individuals in the community sometimes work for the lender, who deducts the loan payments from their daily wages. In such cases no interest is charged.
Loan types	
Among the formal loans that survey respondents reported having taken are housing loans, business loans, vehicle or transport loans, overdrafts, education loans, personal loans, government employee loans, equipment loans, and agricultural loans (such as for farm tools, orchard development, livestock purchases, and seed and fertilizer).	Among the informal loans that survey respondents reported having taken are loans for weddings, religious ceremonies (*pujas*), pilgrimages, payments of other debts, dowries, gambling, bridge financing, and emergencies (illness, death, or natural disasters). Informal loans also include housing loans, business loans, vehicle loans, education loans, equipment loans, and loans for farm development or for the purchase of livestock and other agricultural inputs.

Source: Bhutan Financial Inclusion Focus Group Survey 2012.

Branchless Banking Models for Bhutan

The findings from the Bhutan Financial Inclusion Focus Group Survey suggest that branchless banking through agents is one possible model for extending financial inclusion in the country. Branchless banking allows banks to operate at distance, helping to overcome the high cost barriers in serving remote rural areas. Because the aim is to offer services to marginalized groups that cannot profitably be reached through traditional banking services, branchless banking models developed for this purpose need to be transformational (not just an addition to the range of services offered by banks).

Tarazi and Brelo (2010) have identified several models of branchless banking (figure H.1). Bhutan could benefit most from the development of both bank-based and non-bank-based models.

Several challenges arise in the pioneer phase of developing these innovative services, including technology and costs, business scalability, regulatory barriers, and customer understanding and trust. Field research in Bhutan highlighted large gaps in financial literacy among Bhutanese people. In addition, the survey noted that the use of Internet and mobile phone technology is limited by content issues (the predominance of English, too few subjects of interest, and the like). And ensuring the security and reliability of electronic money as well as overcoming the lack of trust in virtual funds would take time.

These findings suggest that branchless banking in Bhutan should not be limited to a non-bank-based model in which a mobile network operator offers services (including bill payments, cash-in and cash-out services, and domestic money transfers) using agents as a distribution channel, but should also include bank-based models. Indeed, achieving the uptake of non-bank-based models that use electronic money and rely on both mobile phones and agents as delivery platforms (similar to M-Pesa or Orange Money) will be a bigger challenge. Allowing the development of both types of models would help create a level playing field for transformational financial service providers, giving these

Figure H.1 Branchless Banking Models

Source: Tarazi and Brelo 2010, 2.
Note: SBI = State Bank of India.

providers the choice of a wide range of business models and partnerships to profitably serve remote areas.

Financial service providers could use small stores or businesses owning several outlets as agents for delivering branchless banking services. They could also use networks as a distribution channel, such as the postal network.[1] The financial service providers will need to ensure that agents receive adequate training in handling cash and managing liquidity and that measures are in place to protect consumers.

Indeed, innovative services always carry risks for consumers as well as for the service providers and regulatory authorities. While attempting to minimize risks and protect consumers, regulatory authorities should nevertheless ensure that they are not stifling innovation by imposing strong regulatory barriers. Important consumer protection issues include price transparency, technology failures, fraud, data privacy, judiciary risk, agent illiquidity, and insolvency. The agency contract between a financial service provider and its agents should be very clear about the allocation of responsibility. There should be only one entity to turn to if a problem arises, and the financial service provider should be held responsible for all actions of its agents.

The Royal Monetary Authority is drafting new regulations for electronic money issuers (nonbanks) that would apply to a mobile network operator willing to offer non-bank-based branchless banking services. The institution is also preparing regulations for agents of financial service providers, to be enacted in the near future, that would apply to all financial institutions as well as future non-deposit-taking microfinance institutions and electronic money issuers willing to use a network of agents as another channel of distribution for financial services.

To allow the uptake of innovations, especially in the pioneer phase of development, new regulations need to be open and certain. In addition, restrictions need to be kept proportional to risks. For example, measures related to customers' identification need to be kept light in countries where identification cards and formal addresses may be nonexistent, especially in rural areas.

Note

1. According to Bhutan Post's website, its network consists of 89 outlets, including 2 general post offices and 17 post offices. In addition, Bhutan Post has a network of runners who deliver mail and remittance services (Bhutan Postal Corporation, "About Bhutan Post," http://www.bhutanpost.com.bt/index.php?id=32). A financial service provider could replicate this network for its own network of agents or use it directly (under a partnership agreement).

Reference

Tarazi, M., and P. Brelo. 2010. "Nonbank E-money Issuers: Regulatory Approaches to Protecting Customer Funds." CGAP Focus Note 63, Consultative Group to Assist the Poor, Washington, DC. http://www.cgap.org/gm/document-1.9.45715/FN_63_Rev.pdf.

Bibliography

Allen, H. 2002. *CARE International's Village Savings & Loan Programmes in Africa: Micro Finance for the Rural Poor That Works.* https://www.msu.edu/unit/phl/devconference/CAREVillSavLoanAfr.pdf.

Basu, P. 2004. *Improving Access to Finance for India's Rural Poor.* Washington, DC: World Bank. http://www-wds.worldbank.org/servlet/WDSContentServer/IW3P/IB/2006/06/14/000090341_20060614163818/Rendered/PDF/364480PAPER0IN101OFFICIAL0USE0ONLY1.pdf.

CARE. 2011. *Microfinance in Africa: State-of-the-Sector Report—Closing the Gap.* http://www.care.org/getinvolved/advocacy/access-africa/pdf/CARE-Access-Africa-Closing-the-Gap-2011.pdf.

CGAP (Consultative Group to Assist the Poor). 2004. "Key Principles of Microfinance." http://www.cgap.org/sites/default/files/CGAP-Consensus-Guidelines-Key-Principles-of-Microfinance-Jan-2004.pdf.

———. 2010. "Global Standard-Setting Bodies and Financial Inclusion for the Poor: Toward Proportionate Standards and Guidance." http://www.cgap.org/publications/global-standard-setting-bodies-and-financial-inclusion-poor.

Collins, D., N. Jentzsch, and R. Mazer. 2011. "Incorporating Consumer Research into Consumer Protection Policy Making." Focus Note 74, CGAP, Washington, DC. http://www.cgap.org/gm/document-1.9.55701/FN74.pdf.

Demirgüç-Kunt, A., T. Beck, and P. Honohan. 2008. *Finance for All? Policies and Pitfalls in Expanding Access.* Washington, DC: World Bank. http://siteresources.worldbank.org/INTFINFORALL/Resources/4099583-1194373512632/FFA_book.pdf.

Demirgüç-Kunt, A., and L. Klapper. 2012. "Measuring Financial Inclusion: The Global Findex Database." Policy Research Working Paper 6025, World Bank, Washington, DC. http://www-wds.worldbank.org/servlet/WDSContentServer/WDSP/IB/2012/04/19/000158349_20120419083611/Rendered/PDF/WPS6025.pdf.

Ferrari, A. 2008. *Increasing Access to Rural Finance in Bangladesh: The Forgotten "Missing Middle."* Washington, DC: World Bank. https://openknowledge.worldbank.org/handle/10986/6832.

Ferrari, A., G. Jaffrin, and S. R. Shrestha. 2007. *Access to Financial Services in Nepal.* Washington, DC: World Bank. http://siteresources.worldbank.org/NEPALEXTN/Resources/publications/415830-1174327112210/complete.pdf.

Financial Access Survey. 2011. International Monetary Fund, Washington, DC. http://fas.imf.org/.

Galay, K. 2001. "Bhutanese Context of Civil Society." *Journal of Bhutan Studies* 3 (1): 199–218.

Global Financial Inclusion (Global Findex) Database. World Bank, Washington, DC. http://www.worldbank.org/globalfindex.

GPFI (Global Partnership for Financial Inclusion). 2011. "G20 Principles for Innovative Financial Inclusion." http://www.gpfi.org/sites/default/files/documents/G20%20 Principles%20for%20Innovative%20Financial%20Inclusion%20-%20AFI%20 brochure.pdf.

Grant, W. J., and C. A. Henry. 2007. "CARE's Mata Masu Dubara (Women on the Move) Program in Niger: Successful Financial Intermediation in the Rural Sahel." *Journal of Microfinance* 4 (2): 189–216.

Gross National Happiness Commission. 1999. *Bhutan 2020: A Vision for Peace, Prosperity and Happiness.* Thimphu: Gross National Happiness Commission.

Hamid Hussein, M. 2009. "State of Microfinance in Bhutan." Paper prepared for project on State of Microfinance in SAARC Countries, Institute of Microfinance, Dhaka. http://www.inm.org.bd/saarc/document/Bhutan.pdf.

Hess, U., E. Bryla, and J. Nash. 2005. *Rural Finance Innovations: Topics and Case Studies.* World Bank, Washington, DC. http://www.ruralfinance.org/fileadmin/templates/rflc/ documents/1122821975489_RFI_worldbank.pdf.

Hinz, R. 2011. "Financial Capability Toolkit: Project Concept Note." Human Development Network, World Bank, Washington, DC.

Holzmann, R. 2010. "Bringing Financial Literacy and Education to Low and Middle Income Countries: The Need to Review, Adjust, and Extend Current Wisdom." Social Protection Discussion Paper 1007, Human Development Network, World Bank, Washington, DC. http://siteresources.worldbank.org/SOCIALPROTECTION/ Resources/SP-Discussion-papers/Social-Protection-General-DP/1007.pdf.

IFC (International Finance Corporation). 2011. "Financial Inclusion Data: Assessing the Landscape and Country-Level Target Approaches." Discussion paper prepared on behalf of the Global Partnership for Financial Inclusion. Washington, DC. http:// www.gpfi.org/sites/default/files/documents/WORKINGDATA.pdf.

———. 2011. "Measuring Financial Inclusion: Core Set of Financial Inclusion Indicators." AFI Policy Note, Alliance for Financial Inclusion, Bangkok. http://www.afi-global.org/ sites/default/files/afi%20fidwg%20report.pdf?op=Download.

———. 2011. "SME Finance Policy Guide." Paper prepared on behalf of the Global Partnership for Financial Inclusion. Washington, DC. http://www.gpfi.org/sites/ default/files/documents/SME%20Finance%20Policy%20Guide.pdf.

Johnson, S., E. Anyango, E. Esipisu, M. Malkamaki, C. Musoke, and L. Opoku. 2007. "Village Savings and Loan Associations: Experience from Zanzibar." *Small Enterprise Development Journal* 18 (1): 11–24.

Kloeppinger-Todd, R. 2005. "Meeting Development Challenges: Renewed Approaches to Rural Finance." World Bank, Washington, DC. http://www.ruralfinance.org/fileadmin/ templates/rflc/documents/1124790789977_WBank_Meeting_Development_ Challenges.pdf.

Ministry of Labour and Human Resources of the Royal Government of Bhutan. 2011. *Labour Force Survey Report 2011.* Department of Employment, Thimphu.

Niang, C., T. Nenova, and A. Ahmad. 2009. "Bringing Finance to Pakistan's Poor: A Study on Access to Finance for the Underserved and Small Enterprises." World Bank, Washington, DC. http://siteresources.worldbank.org/INTFR/Resources/Paper- NenovaNiangandAhmad.pdf.

NSB (National Statistics Bureau). 2006. *Results of Population & Housing Census of Bhutan 2005*. Thimphu: NSB.

———. 2008. *Socio-Economic and Demographic Indicators 2005*. Thimphu: NSB.

———. 2009. *Statistical Yearbook of Bhutan 2009*. Thimphu: NSB.

———. 2011. *Statistical Yearbook of Bhutan 2011*. Thimphu: NSB.

———. Forthcoming. *Bhutan Living Standard Survey 2012 Report*. Thimphu: NSB.

NSB (National Statistics Bureau) and World Bank. 2010. *Small Area Estimation of Poverty in Rural Bhutan*. Technical Report, NSB, Thimphu, and Economic Policy and Poverty Unit, South Asia Region, World Bank, Washington, DC.

Pain, A., and D. Pema. 2004. "The Matrilineal Inheritance of Land in Bhutan." *Contemporary South Asia* 13 (4): 421–35.

Pickens, M., D. Porteous, and S. Rotman. 2009. "Scenarios for Branchless Banking in 2020." Focus Note 57, CGAP, Washington, DC. http://www.cgap.org/gm/document-1.9.40599/FN57.pdf.

Porter, B. 2011. "National Strategies: Where Do They Get Us? A Roadmap for Financial Inclusion." United Nations Capital Development Fund, New York. http://www.globalmicrocreditsummit2011.org/userfiles/file/Workshop%20Papers/B_%20Porter%20-%20National%20Strategies.pdf.

RMA (Royal Monetary Authority of Bhutan). 2012. *Annual Report 2010/11*. Thimphu: RMA.

———. 2012. "Supply-Side Access to Finance: Key Findings." Paper Presented at a meeting of the Financial Inclusion Policy Working Group, Thimphu, April.

Tarazi, M., and P. Brelo. 2010. "Nonbank E-money Issuers: Regulatory Approaches to Protecting Customer Funds." CGAP Focus Note 63, Consultative Group to Assist the Poor, Washington, DC. http://www.cgap.org/gm/document-1.9.45715/FN_63_Rev.pdf.

UNCDF (United Nations Capital Development Fund) and UNDESA (United Nations Department of Economic and Social Affairs). 2006. *Building Inclusive Financial Sectors for Development*. New York: United Nations. http://www.uncdf.org/sites/default/files/Download/bluebook_0.pdf.

World Bank. 2010. *Bhutan Investment Climate Assessment Report: Vitalizing the Private Sector, Creating Jobs*. South Asia Region, World Bank, Washington, DC. http://documents.worldbank.org/curated/en/2010/09/16409092/bhutan-investment-climate-assessment-report-vitalizing-private-sector-creating-jobs-vol-1-2-volume-summary-report.

———. 2011. *Migration and Remittances Factbook*. 2nd ed. Washington, DC: World Bank.

———. 2011. *World Development Report 2012: Gender Equality and Development*. Washington, DC: World Bank.

———. 2012. *Financial Inclusion Strategies—Reference Framework*. Washington, DC: World Bank. http://siteresources.worldbank.org/EXTFINANCIALSECTOR/Resources/282884-1339624653091/8703882-1339624678024/8703850-1339624695396/FI-Strategies-ReferenceFramework-FINAL.pdf.